Notes
from the
Horn

Notes from the Horn
An anthology of newspaper columns
1977 to 2003

Hale O'Malley

with **Roger O'Malley,** who started it all as
Cornucopia's
and the South Shore correspondent all those years ago.

Savage Press
Superior, Wisconsin

Notes from the Horn
by Hale O'Malley
with Roger O'Malley

Copyright © 2003 by Hale O'Malley

First Edition

Published by Savage Press
P.O. Box 115
Superior, Wisconsin 54880
www.savagepress.com
(715) 394-9513
Printed in the U.S.A.

Editor: Eric Hjerstedt Sharp

Special thanks to *The County Journal*, 324 W. Bayfield St., Washburn, WI 54891 and to its publisher, Gary Pennington, and editor Darrell Pendergrass, to Carlos J. Licea, night editor at The Ashland *Daily Press*, and to Michelle Rosa Sharp.

The County Journal

All rights reserved. No part of this book may be reproduced or transmitted in any form without permission from the author and publisher.

Library of Congress Catalog Card Number 2003110329
ISBN 1-88602861-3

Editor's Notes

Traditionally, small town newspapers have had correspondents who have reported on happenings and events in the outlying communities away from the hustle and bustle of the city newsroom with its "hard news" and street beats.

Hale O'Malley, and his older brother, Roger O'Malley, before him, typify that weekly correspondent who writes from the home often about immediate friends and family and the comings and goings of guests, social affairs and society events of varying importance.

Both O'Malley brothers have taken this a step further, and have designed a stage to include their unique takes on life up north — as far as you can get in the American Heartland — without taking a plunge in the cold, clear waters of the World's largest lake: Lake Superior.

Weekly papers are still a part of the American scene, as are their correspondents who labor diligently for little pay, but must keep the same strict deadlines as staff writers, who work out of the news office. Most correspondents, or society editors as they are sometimes called, take their role as journalists as serious as staff news reporters do, writing and re-writing copy to inform and entertain. Most editors must trust these correspondents' accuracy as much, if not more than their staff writers, merely because they travel in different circles and cover different events. In most cases, the correspondent is the expert in his specific coverage area, and that's what makes him important.

Hale O'Malley's columns have arrived at their respective newspapers like clockwork for decades, as have Roger O'Malley's. Writing for *The Bayfield Press*, (later the *Bayfield County Press*), the *Washburn Times* and lastly *The County Journal,* both writers have captured the essence of the Lake Superior South Shore community of Cornucopia and their specific environ of nearby Bark Bay, a microcosm of the larger Bayfield Peninsula, and a "horn" of land where the column, in part, gets its name; the more obvious "horn of plenty" connotation completing the double meaning. To some extent, the brothers also kept their readers abreast of happenings in the cities of Washburn, where Hale's wife, Marion (Corning) grew up, a descendent of the earliest merchant there; and Bayfield, where both brothers were born and schooled. Their father Joe O'Malley was the local bank president in Bayfield. After graduation from high school, both sons left the small, northernmost Wisconsin city to pursue sales careers.

The lure of The Great Lake, life-long friends and family-ties, deep sea fishing and a love of boating and the surrounding "forest primeval" brought back both brothers, this time just up the road to the one-of-a-kind fishing village of Cornucopia. Hale and Roger, both salesmen, moved back to their home country to set up a real estate sales office, where they sold agates, dispensed information on the South Shore region of Lake Superior and occasionally sold land and homes.

Roger, four years older than Hale, began writing his column "The Scene on 13," and later started the "Notes From The Horn" series, bringing his own brand of humor to readers of the *Bayfield County Press* and *Washburn Times*. Hale took over from him, first writing "Sun Spots" and later filling in for the "Notes From the Horn," which he continues to pen from his desk in Phoenix, Arizona.

Readers look forward to Hale's column each week, and after decades of keeping them in the know, he has developed a sort of distinct style all his own. Whether its about the people of Bayfield or Cornucopia, fishing on Lake Superior or Hale's favorite topic of the Lake Superior Glacial Kettles; the O'Malleys are the kind of writers who have developed their own voices. As Hale so often said: "It's a wonderful world."

Step back, come up north and enjoy the read.

Eric Hjerstedt Sharp, editor, Ashland, Wisconsin, 2003

Author's Preface

I've decided to gather up many of my columns of the past decades, and have an editor pick from the best and send the manuscript off to a publisher to make a book. With the help of Nancy Raeburn who saved some of my columns, Barb Jonas who saved all of Roger's and some of my really old ones from Arizona called Sun Spots, Red Anderson and Mike Coughlin of Cornucopia, and *The County Journal's* Eric Sharp, I hope to get out the book and call it, of course, *Notes From The Horn*.

So when people ask me what I do, I can say 'I'm an author.' Might have to raise a beard, smoke a pipe and wear a beret.

When you're doing your own publishing you can do this: I'm including a story I wrote 35 years ago, "A Real Girl" inspired by a magazine article describing a lady editor you may recognize, a type I can't stand.

The girl is my invention, the editor is real, though I wish it were the other way around.

The other story, about being picked up while hitch-hiking in 1944 by Clark Gable, is fact. Everything else, except the "Sun Spots" columns written from Arizona, is pure South Shore.

— **Hale O'Malley**

CONTENTS

Editor's Note

Preface by Hale

Hale O'Malley: The Early Columns
Sun Spots

Roger O'Malley

Hale's Later Columns:
Notes From The Horn

Glacial Kettles

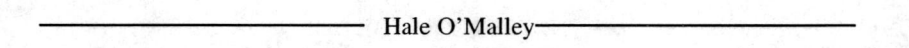

Hale O'Malley

NOTES FROM THE HORN

Half a Tail & Jackass Flats
"Sun Spots," July 1977

    Roger likes to write about his cats, Vincent and Vincenta, and I can understand that; two black blobs in a thousand square miles of white do sort of stand out I suppose and in truth I never had anything against either of those black blotches but we really never had much in common. Fact is we never did hit it off.

    Never mind. We have a cat here, if it's cats you're looking for, who understands and lives by the Creed of Catitude. And this here cat, now, is no common cat. This cat was born in Cornucopia, Wisconsin, Aug. 4, 1977 (Marion says it was Aug. 4, and if Marion says it was Aug. 4, it was Aug. 4) and was given to us by a nice lady who worked at Ehler's store that summer, June Davies. We named him Rip (and so help me, this very moment he came in to rub against my leg and tell me I'm a fine fellow but the service is terrible. Cats always claim the service is terrible).

    We brought Rip down here to Phoenix when he was two months old, and I still remember feeding him bits of Poncho's smoked salmon on the floor of the car as we drove, and if you reached down pretending to steal a little chunk his paw would flash out with five wicked little claws and you were lucky to get away with your life.

    He was born with half a tail and Marion tells everyone "He's a Manx" and as a veteran married man I kept quiet, but the fact is he's just a bob-tailed cat. The crazy thing is that Marion feeds him and babies him, and he won't give her the time of day, but thinks I'm the greatest thing since hamburger. Who can explain this? Not me. Now here he comes again, wants his ears rubbed.

    Cats.

    I was glad to see that Roger's pursuit of "Winter Blues" brought results, not only of the names of all the great musicians pictured on the cover (and that trumpet on the floor in front of Johnny Saylers, Johnny himself GAVE me, 20 years later and 40 years ago) but the verse and chorus to the whole thing, thanks to Chick Sheridan whose like should he ever leave us, will not be seen again.

Roger spent one long winter here on the tract at Prescott where I bought some land 12 years ago, the tract is called Lynx Lake Estates, there being a lake the size of your hat five miles from it where somebody thought they saw a lynx one time, but the original name of this land was Jackass Flats.

Honest. So he composed this verse to the Music of Winter Blues:

"*It ain't no joke I'm going bats*
 Living here on Jackass Flats
  Gee it's hell to try to sell
  A lot
  That God forgot.
  Crickets, snakes and cactus thorn
  Here's where sheep like us are shorn
  It stinks, Jake,
  At Lynx Lake
  I've got the Jackass Blues"

All together now fellows, one more time: It ain't no joke I'm going bats...

But this Way Lies Madness

Some days I feel like Huckleberry Finn: "I'm always held back," he said, "I never get no show." Here I've read the Nov. 13 issue of "Notes From the Horn" and counted five times where Roger wrote Grossbeak when of course the bird's name is spelled Grosbeak, and I was all set to nail his hide to the barn door right here when in the last paragraph he saved himself.

"It should be noted," he writes, "that the word grossbeak should be spelled with only one "s". "Grosbeak" although their beaks are really gross and I prefer the two s's. I suspect he looked that up the last minute and tacked that paragraph on just in time to save himself; just the same I feel cheated. I'm always held back. I never get no show. It's a cloudy day here too. Rats.

I've just ordered two tickets to the play "Annie" and you know what they charge? Eighteen bucks each. Talk about inflation! I suppose I could cancel the order, but it's Marion's birthday and how can you say "I know it's your birthday but the tickets are too expensive and I never liked that comic strip anyway?" You can't do that, can you? Of course not, that would be absolutely gross. As in beak.

I've just signed up for another course in Spanish, a language that has eluded me for years, but probably I'd be smarter to stick to figuring out English. You can do so much with English, for example, I've just received a bill from the Apostle Islands Marina in Bayfield, coming when I was just catching my breath from the price of those tickets to "Annie." Would it be correct to say that when you get a stiff bill from a marina, that you feel marinated? (Marinate: to let stand in oil and vinegar, my dictionary says.)

Yes, I think that fits. I can hear Jim saying, "Marge, Christmas is coming, gotta lot of presents to buy, let's marinate a few dozen more today."

I could go on, but this way lies madness. Besides the sun is coming out and I've got to get on my bicycle and peddle up to 35th Avenue and put this in the mail.

Hang the Expense!

BAYFIELD — I see by the *Times* (Washburn, not New York — there's nothing interesting in *The New York Times* — besides it's too thick) that John Boehme just made a set of steps for kids too small to reach up for their library books. It's like John to do that and I'm sure he'd have done it back when I was too small to reach up to that desk, except that when I was too small so was he.

The last time John and I met was last summer in Bodin's Fish House where he was selecting some special fishbits for his cat. Just like him to do that too. Our cat, Clancy, has to eat out of cans and he hates the stuff and grumbles and gripes all the time. Marion tries to fool him by switching brands but he says he doesn't care what's on the label, it's the same gooey mess inside every time. No matter. Show me a cat that isn't constantly complaining about the food and the service and what you've got there, friend, is a sick cat.

Ah, the Bayfield Library. Many a pleasant hour passed there, and I remember so well the Robinson sisters who were the librarians, quiet, gentle ladies who I think came with the building. They spoke in the softest voices, as born librarians do, and I am trying now to picture them talking any other way, anywhere. To picture one of the Robinson sisters suddenly letting out a yell is — well, the very thought is blasphemy, that's what it is. I'm sorry I even mentioned it.

The next time you go to the library take a look at the low concrete wall that borders the steps. It's about a foot-and-a-half wide, and two neat parallel grooves are worn in the center, the whole length of them, especially the one on your left as you walk up.

Those grooves were made over the years, by hundreds and hundreds of Bayfield kids sliding down them and wearing out their shoes in the process and I want you to know I did my part. What would the Red Front, Nelson's and McCredie's stores have done without us? In our little way we kept them in business, and small thanks we got for it too and none whatsoever from our folks. Well doggonit, we had to do the sliding, all our folks had to do was buy the shoes. Life is unfair.

I made it a point last summer to walk up and check those grooves and they're right there, in good shape, maybe a hair deeper than when I last slid down that wall about 60 years ago. I think next summer I'll sneak back up there some dark night and slide down just once more. Yessir, that's what I'll do. I'll buy a pair of new shoes with shiny leather soles and leather heels — you have to have leather heels, you know that — and some dark quiet night when nobody's around — hang the expense! — I'll sneak up there and...

Cathouse for Sale
March 1, 1979

A card just in from Marti Miller, one of my favorite Millers, which reads as follows:

Hale: Webster says: sunspot: one of the dark spots that occasionally appear on the sun's surface commonly like a blue-black umbra with a surrounding penumbra of lighter shade and usually visible only through my telescope, we found what seemed to be lots of sun spots, but they ended up just being several periods and a semicolon. Marti Miller, Marina Manager, winter operations.

Well it's good to know that "Sun Spots" has at least one reader and two counting me, and this is enough to bring me to the typewriter once a week. Marti, by the way, is an artist as well as a marina manager and I enclose a little sketch she made of her dad's great trawler, the *Prime Time*. If it isn't reproduced here call Marti at the Apostle Islands Marina and she'll send it to you.

I can report today that at 11'o'clock this morning, Feb. 23, I put old friend Ron Roman on the American Airlines jet and he will be back in Cornucopia any minute now, fully prepared to tell anyone there that Phoenix in February isn't warm at all and Prescott is worse. I think he had a good time though. He bought us a fine dinner at Crazy Ed's, played me liar's poker that night and lost, played for lunch again the next day, lost again, went to the Elk's Club that night and shook a little dice where he was decent enough to lose once more.

We enjoyed Ron's visit very much, in truth I'd have enjoyed it even if he'd won all those games. There are no freeloaders in the Roman family.

Now I see that Roger's cats Vincent and Vincenta are continuing their sinful ways and are about to deliver another batch of kittens conceived and born without benefit of clergy, the shameless things. WHAT ARE WE COMING TO? I tell you this world's in a bad condition.

This reminds me that a few years ago I worked up an ad for a house I was trying to sell in Mexico, this to appear in the *Phoenix Republic*, a very stuffy paper. This ad was to read "For sale, five Mexican kittens, $35,000; deal including two-story, three-bedroom house. OWN YOUR OWN CATHOUSE IN SUNNY MEXICO!"

On the opposite page this paper had an ad for the movie "Deep Throat" but do you suppose they'd print my little want ad? Not them. I went in to see about it and a prickly-faced old gal at the desk said, "Why we can't print that, Mr. O'Malley." I said, sweetly, "You know you have an ad on the opposite page for a show I would not even let these kittens see?"

"That's not my department," she said, and that was that. I sold the house anyway, a little later, and gave away thirty-five thousand dollars worth of kittens. Plain threw away $35,000, but what the heck. Ron will be back next winter.

Twenty Gallons of Diesel Fuel in her Tank
Sun Spots, June 14, 1979

The lion in the circle is just a picture, the one showing us what fine teeth he has is real. Then, left to right, we have Marion O'Malley, Hale O'Malley (well in back and braced for a quick getaway), Judy and Bill Mangino.

This was taken at the huge MGM Hotel in Las Vegas; they have had the lion on display every day and by now he must have had his picture taken with a million tourists. There is absolutely nothing between him and the people except a keeper with a stick. I think the keeper was as bored as the lion. I saw him yawn too, but of course, the lion had it all over him for teeth. We didn't check either one of them for claws, we went back to the blackjack table and got properly clawed by the dealer, who also had a nice set of teeth. All those guys do.

A nice phone call the other day from Mr. Jack Buehler, whose name I'm probably spelling wrong; Mr. Buehler lives at Sun City but has lived in Bayfield and will be back there this summer. I look forward to meeting him, particularly since he called just to say he read this column and more particularly because he said he knew Lida Rose. So I've yet to meet him but already I like him twice.

This fellow Bill Mangino, by the way, is also an avid reader of the WASHBURN TIMES. Not just for Sun Spots or Notes From the Horn, he reads the whole thing and he's never even been to Washburn. (Well, he drove through on the way to the Cornucopia Yacht Club Bash a couple of years ago but that's all). And here he was born in Phoenix, the only person I've met who actually was born there, come to think of it.

All right. Tomorrow we throw caution to the winds and start for Bayfield by way of California and Seattle. I'm anxious to get back to the *Lida Rose*; I love that little boat and besides that there's 20 gallons of diesel fuel in her tank and I have to stand guard over it.

Driven Over the Edge of the World

Friend Art Johnson, transplanted St. Paul attorney who has been in Phoenix for 26 years which makes him more of a native than half the population here, has two nephews, age 8 and 10, half Korean, and all-American. The other day they came over looking for work.

"Got anything for us to do around here Uncle Art?"

"Let's see. Hmm. Yeah, how about piling up that firewood for me? Give you a dollar apiece."

"O.K. Hey, wait a minute. You sure you got enough money to pay us? There must be a hundred pieces there!"

Koreagate on your doorstep.

About a week from now Marion and I and Spare Parts head for Bayfield and Cornucopia by way of Seattle and Canada so if you never hear from us again you'll understand. Funny thing, bombarded with daily reports on the gas situation as we are, we still have to see for ourselves. The newspapers, TV, radio, the government and the oil companies tell us all about it every day and still we know nothing. I've decided that if any of those people really do know anything they're either keeping it to themselves or lying about it.

Where to turn for the truth, dear reader? Why, right here of course. I will tell you the truth, the whole truth, the truthity-truth-truth and if the truth doesn't set you free it may at least convince you not to drive from Phoenix to Cornucopia by way of Seattle. Watch this column! If one day soon it turns up absolutely blank you will know that the world is flat after all, and we have driven over the edge.

Or just plain run out of gas.

Let me back up a little here. I just remembered that I promised some time back to tell you about our trip through the Bahamas with Jim and Marge Miller last winter, on their great trawler the "Prime Time." And I held off, thinking it is a plain dirty trick or worse than that maybe we wouldn't be allowed back on Lake Superior at all.

Now at this writing I have it on good authority that the ice is out at last and that as the Burma Shave signs used to say:

Spring has Sprung,
The grass has riz
Where last year's
Careless driver Is

So I won't bore you with more words about the Bahamas but I'm enclosing a snapshot which the TIMES might print at the top of this column. It looks like the gang on the Prime Time are at anchor southwest of Eagle Island with Bark Point off to the left, but that is Square Rock in the Bahamas, Feb. 4, 1979.

There. I won't say another word about it.

Ripped Off 1979

We have been ripped off. That is to say we let our cat Rip off the *Lida Rose* one night a week ago "accidentally" and haven't seen him since, and as far as we know nobody else has either. Where do cats disappear to anyway? Here we are all set to take a long trip around Keweenaw Peninsula and can't move, and it's all his fault.

You'll see an ad for him in this issue and I hope he shows up somewhere and we get him back. We really like that cat, troublesome as he is, and we sure want to see him again but believe me I'm going to cut down on his ration of Tender Vittles at least until we recover the cost of the ad. And he's got to realize there's only room for one captain on the *Lida Rose* and he isn't it. On the other hand, maybe he is; everything's gone haywire here since he left. Come back Rip! All is forgiven!

We've just come from a highly unusual party on the beach at Cornucopia. A quiet fellow named Bill Patterson "Wild Bill" they called him used to be seen around Poncho's, sipping a little wine and bothering nobody; he died a few months ago. Suddenly we learn from his attorney Gary Sherman of Port Wing that he had left five hundred dollars to be spent on a party for his friends. That party was held on Marten's Beach Sunday afternoon and I presume on into Sunday evening and for all I know it's going yet. I know very little about Wild Bill but I know when he left, he left in style. He'll be remembered.

A few years ago a gentleman named Gil Larson, no longer with us, created, not single-handedly, but almost, something he called a Nature Trail in the big ravine which runs almost into downtown Bayfield and which used to furnish us our floods (1926, 1942 and 1946); after clawing its way back from that last one Bayfield got money somewhere to build a big pipeline to divert the water and things have been quiet ever since. Where was I? — well, Gil created that Nature Trail through the ravine up to the remains of the old dam which I've crossed a thousand times on the way to school, and I walked it the other day.

If it weren't for the heavy planks and the series of steps, you'd never get through, even if you walked the bed of the little stream. But the walk is just difficult enough to be a challenge, and it's beautiful there. I think you should walk it alone. I did, and when I got to the old dam the trail led up the bank to the school, exactly the route I used to take, and there's a white pine still there that years ago someone had wound barbed wire around. You can still see the lines in the bark, just as they were the last time I made that trip years, years ago.

Remember Ray Cahill the barber?

"Give me the same haircut you've been giving me for forty years," I said.

"You mean fifty."

"FIFTY!?"

"Yes, fifty. I started with Jack Moon in 1929 where the hardware store is now and I cut your hair then. Subtract 29 from 79. Fifty, right?"

Right. Good Grief. And he still has the old clock stopped dead at 9:15 with the sign above it, "What Difference Does It Make?"

I hope he and that clock and sign go back another fifty. At least.

Times A'Changin at Personnel

Just reviewed the April 12 issue of the TIMES and came across two items that would have shocked me if I had any shockability left.
Item #1:
The personnel committee of the Bayfield County Board will receive applications for the position of a full-time County Extension Office Secretary. Starting date will be on or about May 1, 1979.

Desirable Qualifications: High School education with additional vocational or college secretarial training and at least one year within the last three of office experience.

Shorthand-70 words per minute, Typing-55 words per minute.

Salary Range: Starting monthly salary-$727 in 6 months $761, 18 months-$795. There will be a cost-of-living salary adjustment effective April 1, 1979, and quarterly thereafter.

Item #2, from the Washburn Times, dated April 6, 1939: Applications are now being filed for the position of Bayfield County Service Officer with a salary of $1,200 per year.

Well, as Johnny Sayles used to say, "Times dew change!" They sure do, and now I'm wondering who got that juicy post of Service Officer at $100 a month and could it have been our old friend Tom Anderson, or was that before he came in? Probably was, I think he would have been getting ready to take on World War II that year, same as the rest of us, though none of us knew it.

How well I remember sitting in a little coffee shop in Seattle with my friend Rudy Verral in 1939, and you can bet your laughing blue eyes I'm not going to try passing along the advice of Tom Anderson whom I grew up with, which was "Be sure to set something aside for a rainy day!"

I don't know about Tom, but I did that, and sit here fully prepared to get through that rainy day, provided it quits raining about 8:30 a.m.

Your Compass Knows the Way
Sun Spots 1980
> *"A foggy day in London Town*
> *Had me gloomy and had me down."*

Not London this time: Bayfield, and as I sit here on the Aura Lee I can just see the end of the pier, beyond that it's one great gray pillow and any boats out in it are wishing they were somewhere else.

Last night Chick Sheridan and Flutta Ungrodt stopped by to let me brag about this beautiful boat as though I'd built it myself and we took a run over to the Pub for a good trout dinner and came back at slow speed through the murkiest murk you've ever seen. Alfred Hitchcock himself couldn't have whomped up a spookier setting, and what made it even spookier was you knew there were other boats out there with you, unheard, unseen. Just as blind as you and if they had any sense, just as nervous.

Of course you slow down from time to time to sound a few blasts on the horn (and once we got an answering blast from a boat we never saw and didn't want to) and you keep one eye ahead and one on the compass which from La Pointe to Bayfield is 225 degrees and even in that short three-mile run there's a moment when your built-in personal radar says the harbor entrance is over THERE at the same time the compass is saying, "No, it's to the left, over THERE." And you don't want to believe it.

I wouldn't have the nerve to even mention this except that it's probably common to everyone who's ever run a boat in the fog. The compass says" You're ten degrees north, but, pull her back to 335 degrees," and you say "Yeah, but I just know it's over THAT way," – and after all, who's that running this boat, you or some fool compass? And it's all you can do to follow orders and steer 335 degrees by a compass just corrected scientifically by Master Mariner Gil Porter who knew what he was doing, so your compass knows what it's doing, and furthermore your personal built-in radar isn't worth a hoot and never was. Leave that to homing pigeons and sockeye salmon.

We hit the harbor right on the nose.

I think my memory's failing too. When Wally and I were weathered in for a day at Whitefish Point, 30 miles this side of the Soo Locks, we talked with Mr. Tom Brown, 84, who is still mad at Solly Boutin for cheating him out of seven tons of coal in 1917. He said the old tug R.T. Roy, which all Bayfield kids, respecting nothing, called the Rotten Tug Roy, had belonged to his father who'd sold it to Solly. Off and on, through the past half-century, I've wondered who the original R.T. Roy was, and I never thought to ask Mr. Brown about it. I'll drop him a line today, if I don't forget. He's probably the only person alive who knows.

Ugly Dog Contest

I am sorry to have to report that our little Mexican dog "Cringe" is no longer with us. She was with us every day for some 11 years and we'll sure miss her, but old age took her quietly and painlessly two days ago.

She was given to us by a Mexican friend who found her in the desert where of course she wouldn't have lasted more than a few days and you had only to look at her to have her collapse in despair, begging for mercy. You'd have thought we whipped her three times a day to see that act of hers but it really wasn't an act, it was just her nature. So Cringe was a natural name for her though our beach neighbor Ray Dees called her "Spare Parts" which fitted her too, so she went by both.

Of course any animal lucky enough to fall into Marion's hands could just lie back, relax and be waited on the rest of its life; we've had a half dozen cats who'd testify to that, or rather they would if there was an ounce of decency and gratitude in them but of course cats expect that kind of treatment as their natural right. You can haul in a half-starved cat, de-louse him, clean him up and feed him on slices of prime rib and two days later he announces there are going to be some changes made around here, and hands you a list.

If you've been around the Apostle Island Marina at Bayfield, you probably met Cringe, she was around there quite a bit the last few summers, poking at people for petting, then going into her don't-hit-me-oh-please-don't-hit-me routine, as though anybody ever did. (Come to think of it, I did give her a rap on the rear once and she ran under the bed and stayed there till I went and apologized, said I was a mean old man and I was sorry I wouldn't do it again, and after awhile she came out. We didn't say any more about it).

Quite often people would study her for some moments, she did look like a little black watermelon on knock-kneed toothpicks, and say you know, "I think that's the ugliest dog I've ever seen." I always bristled a little at that but I realized they only saw her from the outside; they didn't know her like we did. Inside she was beautiful. (As a matter of fact we once entered her in an Ugly Dog Contest here in Phoenix, and she didn't even get Honorable Mention, we did it just to prove a point).

I remember so well those early years in Mexico, before the town got prosperous. We had a little place on the beach and Cringe used to trot along with us, running in about three inches of water, snapping at minnows. Boy how she loved that game, even more than chasing gophers and lizards where we were building houses at Las Conchas. Of course she never caught one gopher, nor a lizard either, and I think when we finally had to leave the beach the minnow score stood: Minnows-1,000,000; Cringe-0.

All right. She sure had a good life and I guess we can't feel too bad about it. I don't think we'll get another dog for quite awhile though.

Lida Rose Rolls & Caramel Rolls

"Who cuts, splits and piles all that nice oak firewood for Roger?"

"Oh, I have a man up from Arizona every year handling that job for me. Good man. Been with me for years."

Boy that's class, isn't it? Bring a woodcutter up from Arizona to put up your next winter firewood for you couldn't possibly find a qualified man around Cornucopia of course. What he doesn't tell you is that man is his brother, me, and the job pays no salary, has one fringe benefit. (Korbel's brandy at 5 p.m. and I'm not a brandy drinker) and offers no retirement plan whatsoever. I would start a union and demand shorter hours and portal-to-portal pay, or something like that, but a one-man union probably doesn't have much clout. And the next thing I'd know, some scab would move in on me and I'd be out of a job. And me five months short of being a Senior Citizen.

The first Junior Citizen around here who calls me a Senior Citizen gets a belt in the puss.

At long last we are back on the *Lida Rose* and it's good to be home, and I am typing this in her combination bedroom and galley as she rolls gently in her berth here at the Apostle Island Marina in Bayfield. Spare Parts snoozing on my bare left foot, tomcat Rip in a little cubbyhole in the bow and I believe they're as happy to be here as Marion and I are. (Both Spare and Rip have their eyes closed but they're listening to every word I write, I can tell that).

I'm sorry to have missed last week's issue, I did write something and mailed it from Medicine Hat, or rather left it in a motel to be mailed and maybe it never was. I know it was Medicine Hat, Alberta, because I mentioned that I started out to hitchhike there 45 years ago just because I liked the name. I never made it, landed in Seattle instead so I felt pretty good finally getting there. It's a nice little city and I still like the name even if they do forget to mail my letters.

I wish to report here that this morning we had breakfast at the

Pier, Jack and Shirley Johnson's fine restaurant at the City Dock, and we were served fresh caramel rolls with real caramel topping on them, not a painting of brown shellac like you usually get. I haven't had a good caramel roll since my mother made them and that's a long time ago. One of the most under-rated pleasures of life is a fresh caramel roll and coffee for breakfast. I mean a caramel roll with caramel on it.

We'll go back tomorrow. And nuts to that foolishness about calories. Phooey on the calories.

Ron Roman is taking his revenge, clipped me for four bucks in liar's poker at Poncho's yesterday. Sacrificed two weeks pay just so he could be back in Cornie when we came in, to take a lousy four bucks off me, Well, O.K., I don't mind losing. I don't mind losing but I hate to pay.

There'll be other days.

I must close on a sad note. We've just attended funeral services for my old friend Andy Polaski, who died at 68 a few days ago. How well I remember when the two of us started the building of the log cabin at Bark Bay. We didn't even own the land but my dad owned a fourth of it and that was toehold enough in those days. That was 33 years ago, and the cabin is still there and we sure had some great times in that place. Bayfield never had a better citizen than Andy, he liked everybody and everybody liked him. We miss him. We'll always miss him.

Do you Still Like Boating, Marion?

Smile Wisconsin! Florida is cold too!

The *Lida Rose*, 25 feet of should-know-better, has chugged from Houston all the way to this wet town of Panama City, Florida on her way to Lake Superior by way of the east coast and as self-appointed Captain I can assure you that a good Wisconsin blizzard is nowhere near as discouraging as eight straight days of Florida drizzle. Cold drizzle. With sharp winds.

We left Fort Walton this morning for the 65-mile run to Panama City through the Intracoastal Canal which in this area is mostly a channel-marked line through West Bay, East Bay, Choctawhatchie Bay and St. Andrews Bay, all part of the Gulf of Mexico, but protected from the main Gulf by long strips of offshore islands.

I had to stand at the wheel with my head out of the open top of *Lida Rose* so I could see where I was going, but this gave the salt spray, helped by a 12-mile-an-hour wind (I'm not salty enough to speak in knots yet) a good shot at my glasses. Of course couldn't see that way so I kept taking them off, but being very near-sighted I couldn't see then either. This really made little difference as with the fog and drizzle I couldn't have seen anything anyway. Fortunately the channel markers are close enough so you catch the one coming up just before you are about to wander off course into the mist, and you lurch from one to the other while you keep one hand on the wheel, one hand and one eye on the chart to note the buoy numbers as they come up, and both ears on the radio weather report.

The same guys who give the weather up there give it here. "Possible thunderstorms ona line from twenty miles easta Norleanns to House Bayou Loosiana. Visibility three miles."

A wall of spray whaps me in the face as I squint ahead for the next channel buoy.

"Temperachers in the low sixties, expected higha sevenny today, colder tonightentomora."

I am shivering and my new Cornucopia Yacht Club jacket is

soaked. I'll be drummed out of the Club sure. "Parly cloudy to cloudy clearing laytinna day." It is already later in the day and the whole world is socked in. "Possible innermitten shars..."

It is pouring now, and I have to close the plastic top which keeps out some of the wind and most of the rain, and I stare through the windshield with my eyes bugged out like Mr. Magoo. Loyal wife Marion and loyal-to-everybody Mexican dog Spare Parts are making the best of it. They even try to smile.

"Do you still like boating, Marion?," I ask witty as ever. "I guess I have to," she says. Spare looks away.

The rain eases for a moment and I open the top to see if I can spot the bridge over the channel this side of Panama City. This triggers another deluge, "A low pressure area cennered over Eas'Texas and Loosiana will bring innermitten shars" I turn the damn thing off.

What's so bad about a good healthy Wisconsin blizzard anyway? I'll never say another word.

Sail Away for $60,000
Sun Spots May 10 1979

I have it!

I have the Solution!

I have the solution to the problem of getting myself appointed to the committee charged with determining the feasibility of building and maintaining a city marina, this committee called, I presume, the Washburn Marina Committee.

Now of course I can't expect as a resident of Phoenix, Arizona, Puerto Penasco, Mexico and sometimes Bayfield and Cornucopia, Wisconsin, to qualify for any such appointment on the basis of Washburn citizenship. I might, though, be hired as a consultant. (I think that should be capitalized. Consultant. There. I feel better).

Twenty-nine years ago I attended a school for life insurance salesmen at the Edgewater Beach Hotel in Chicago — two weeks of it, and I learned there the definition of Consultant — it's the only thing I did learn and the Edgewater Beach doesn't exist anymore, but never mind that.

Here you are: "a Consultant is a man who knows less about your business than you do but who makes more money telling you how to run it than you'd make if you ran it right instead of the way he tells you." Or to narrow it down: "Consultant: an expert in a given field.." "Expert: a man from out of town."

Modesty demands that I here rest my case.

A bit more about marinas. The largest marina in the world, I'm told, is at Los Angeles, California, called Marina Del Rey. I have always wanted to see it and last week had the chance, going over there with attorney Art Johnson who was there to take what lawyers call a deposition, meaning recording on paper some guy's exact answers to a lot of questions to which a year later in court he can refer, to trip the poor devil up. While he was off on this business I had several hours to poke around this huge marina, and it is something.

Would you believe 6,000 boats? Berths for 6,000 and every one occupied; I talked to one of the many brokers whose offices line the shore. "A fellow we know has a berth here, a small one, and has been waiting five years for a 40-footer," he said. Five years. He offered to show me a 34-foot trawler almost exactly like Jim's at Bayfield. Spanking new, a beautiful thing. "I can put you in this boat, sail-away, for sixty thousand dollars," he said as I stood on the polished deck in my stocking feet (no leather soles, boat shoes only please), practically choking back the tears.

"Oh, the sixty thousand would be no problem," I said looking him right in the eye and fooling nobody, "but where would I keep it?"

"Yes, that is a problem," he sighed. "We lost a lot of sales that way."

We smiled sadly,shook hands and went our separate ways, two liars who might never meet again, but who if they did were prepared to deny everything.

I did some serious thinking. Say at a wild guess, that those 6,000 boats were worth an average of only $5,000 each. That's $30,000,000 — thirty million in, say what you will, toys. I talked to the Harbor Master, who said berthing my little Lida Rose, 25', would cost me $100 a month; that's just for a berth and of course no berths are available. So if all boats there were only twenty-five feet, and they aren't, that's $600,000 a month. Now add in the cantina, the restaurant, the motel, the ...oh, nuts.

The Real Thing

Know what I saw downtown today? A girl. A real girl.

Oh, I know, they aren't so rare as all that, you still see them, often enough so you haven't noticed how scarce they're getting. It's like the partridge hunting when you were a kid; it just got poorer and poorer till one day you woke up to the fact that the reason you weren't going hunting much any more was that it wasn't any use: there was nothing left to hunt.

I want to tell you about this girl. She wore a dress. Not slacks, or blue jeans or what they used to call hot pants. A dress. She wore a dress.

I wouldn't want you to think I stared at this girl but when she came around the corner it was like a morning in May. There was a little swirl to her skirt and a neat belt around her waist, and whatever color or style that dress was it fit her without advertising her, if you follow me. It was the kind of dress a girl would wear who wanted to look like a girl. All the time.

She looked so natural, so fresh and nice, so genuine; her own eyelashes, her own eyebrows, and you know what color her lips were? Red. I mean a reasonable, healthy girl red. Not the frightening scarlet you see on these babes on TV, not orange, not coral. Just the kind of color you like to see on a girl's lips; a kind of velvet rosebud. You know what I mean — I mean it can't be *that* long since you've seen a real girl. Is it?

Her hair. It was fixed the way a girl does who knows how to do her hair and put a little wave in it, and it wasn't hanging down her back or over her face, and it wasn't piled up in a heap that you'd expect something to fly out of any minute. It was a nice, rich natural brown too, the color I knew it had started out to be.

Maybe she got to me so because I'd just read a magazine article about a very successful female editor who was described this way — honest — "her philosophy is simple; old-fashioned morality is OUT if it cuts down on the excitement and fun. Affairs and divorces are IN, provided you can handle the problems. Above all, female readers are instructed to be completely and responsibly feminine.

"This code she takes personally to heart, and indeed she seems living proof of its validity. When she receives a male visitor in her office she will smile bashfully, float away from her desk to a couch, curl up her legs, wrap her arms around a pillow, raise her eyebrows and begin talking in a soft very intimate voice about how tiny she is and how she uses a padded bra and pancake makeup and wears a wig and false eyelashes."

Fellows, that isn't our girl. Our girl is natural, and pretty and a lot of fun, and she likes you. You can tell that right away — I knew she liked ME the minute she came round the corner. The wind touched her hair and skirt and she cocked her head a little to one side and gave me a kind of smile that made me feel I'd live to a hundred and never be over twenty seven.

That's what I saw downtown this morning, boys. A real girl. The real thing.

I could weep.

Roger O'Malley

A Solid Citizen
Notes from the Horn

Most of us who now live in small towns like Cornucopia tend to forget what it's like to live in a large city. Here we greet everyone we see, even those few we might not like, and also those we don't know as there is always the chance we might have met them some time or other. In a city one seldom knows or says hello to people who live next door in the same apartment building. People who wait for the bus on the same street corner year after year do not speak and make elaborate attempts not to see each other. This brings us to our feature story of the week about another of our prominent citizens.

No series about Cornucopia people could be complete without a story about our Bill Martens, who is probably the happiest and certainly one of the best loved people in town. And we'll bet he is known to more of our visitors than any of us.

Bill didn't start out with all the advantages most of us have. The medical profession probably has a long word for it, but his capacity for acquiring most of the technical parts of modern civilization such as reading, writing and other such necessary tools is limited. It would seem that such a person couldn't get along in our advanced society but Bill holds his own and then some in Corny.

Bill is not a child, he's older than our average resident, and we tend to overlook many of his activities, we're so familiar with them, but he keeps himself very busy in a number of projects. He helps check out grocery shipments coming into the local store and keeps a running inventory of the stock, although his markings in his workbook are meaningful only to himself.

One of his hobbies is singing with the organist at the local Poncho's Supper Club. Bill oversees the loading of the mail and checks out our local postmaster, Elsie Lawin, and does a good job of supervising and pumping of gas in Reuben's storage tanks. Bill is better known to our visitors as our Sheriff and he wears his star

Roger O'Malley

badge (Sheriff of Cornucopia) with pride and dignity.

   It is true that our local people go a little out of their way to help Bill and make life good for him, but it is also true that he has contributed his share of good humor and friendliness to our town and we feel we're better for it. Bill might have some problems making his way in a larger community but here in Corny he's BILL MARTENS, solid citizen, and we love him.

Both Looking for a Soft Spot

It's been quite a while since we've sounded off about something in this column. It's been too peaceful, so here goes.

A practical joker friend of ours put Hale's name on the mailing list of a racketeer from Fresno, California, name of Rev. Al. This Rev Al isn't a regular con man, for which types we have sort of a tolerant respect. A regular con man rips off greedy people who have lots of money and want to make more easily, such as those movie and television stars who dropped a bundle in shady oil well deals. Rev. Al probably does as well with the dollars but he directs his appeal to those people on the lowest rung of our economic ladder. He asks for $5 for him to bless a small cellophane package of salt.

"Great riches will come to you!" He asks $6.38 so he can plant a small mustard seed for you in the Holy Land to whence he is planning an all expense tour for himself. To make sure you understand the idea he includes a shiny new penny which you should touch to remind you of your financial obligations.

His latest is an impassioned plea addressed to his "Brother Hale" asking for $25 to help finance his junket as his funds are exhausted. He says, "I am making plans to leave the day I hear from you." (With, of course, your $25).

This is all done on a very expensive automatic printing machine which makes every letter look personal, and he must put out thousands of them. He "knows Brother Hale's problems and is heartsick about them." (Don't forget to enclose your $25) He doesn't know any more about Hale than a Lamprey does about a lake trout but they're both looking for a soft touch.

Pictures are shown of people who have sent in their $5, probably borrowed or salvaged from a relief check and who have suddenly come into much cash from some unsuspected source. These people deserve help and consideration and not a blatant rip-off like they are getting from Rev. Al. He also has a lawyer who adds in very, very fine print that Al disclaims responsibility and says it's up to the reader to believe what he says.

We are incensed, and hope the Post Office Department leans on him soon.

Deja Vu

Criticism isn't always nice to receive but it is nice when someone criticizes an item in a column like this. It means someone has read it. We've just had a letter from a lady in the State of Washington. Man do we reach out! This lady objected to our comments about giving away some kittens our Vincenta will soon present us with, and she insists we have her "fixed." (The cat that is).

We don't want to get into any "pro-life" discussion in this little portion of our paper but we do insist on going along with Vincent and Vincenta's plans and we're prepared to take care of the family.

We also had a telephone call from friend Irene Nelson in Port Wing who took us to task for an incorrect quotation. We wrote that a famous philosopher said "A man without a woman is like a fish without a bicycle." We thought it was rather cute but Irene insists it was "A woman without a man is like a fish without a bicycle." We backed off here too and declined to get into a women's lib discussion although in this case we can't see that it makes much difference in meaning whichever way we used the quotation.

They say the French have a word for it and they have a dandy in the word "Deja Vu." My seven-inch thick dictionary lists it and says deja vu is from the French word deja vu. How about that? The only definition listed is the word paramnesia, and that word is defined as "An illusion of remembering scenes and events experienced for the first time." The only reason for bringing this up now is that the word is becoming quite popular lately in columns and in novels although I have yet to hear anyone using it in conversation. If I were to use it in conversation I'd certainly prefer the French one rather than the English one. Paramnesia sounds like a leaky gland or something while deja vu sounds esoteric or exotic or maybe even erotic. If anyone wants to use it in conversation it is pronounced "day-zha-vue" and the French dictionary says it means "already seen."

It sure is tough trying to find something to write about while waiting for spring.

Fish by the Cubic Foot in Pure Lake Superior Water

We may not hear from friend Rodrill Hukenlien for a while, he has struck a bonanza. It seems he was following up his plan to catch smelt with a snow shovel and dip net as reported here a week or so ago. Rodrill and co-worker Remingchester Colt were scooping up smelt by the bushel as they came up through the bobbing hole in Bark Bay and headed for Bark Creek under a layer of snow and over 36 inches of ice. The boys had to leave to replenish their supply of blackberry brandy and when they returned the next day the temperature was three degrees below zero and everything was frozen solid. Hukenlien reports, that there was a solid jam-packed layer of smelt in a regular river from the hole to the creek, frozen solid. Between the two of them they chain sawed out four pick-up truck loads of smelt, packed like sardines and frozen in pure Lake Superior Water.

They plan on selling the fish by the cubic foot and with the price of hamburger what it is, they expect to clean up before the warm weather sets in around the fourth of July.

Notice! Readers who don't like cats please turn the page. (After reading the advertising of course). We reported in February that Vincent and Vincenta would have children on Friday, April 6. This was based on some extensive research done at the Vaughn Library in Ashland where we learned that the gestation period for cats is 63 days.

Knowing the honeymoon date we could forecast with confidence and we hit it on the button, right to the hour. We now have four handsome kittens, two black, two grey. Applications for adoption are stacking up and we are busy checking references, inspecting homes and making sure of financial responsibility to insure the proper environment for Vince and Vincenta's family.

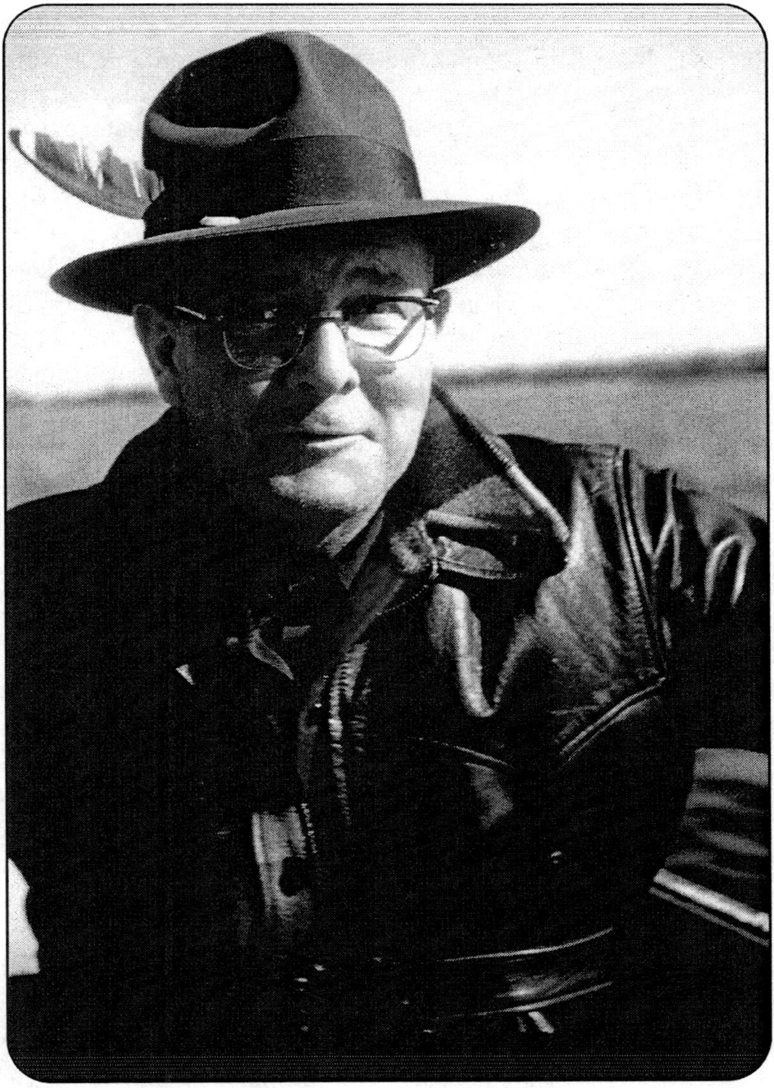

Just The Bear Facts

With all the trouble we've been having here in Cornucopia with our bear, or bears, it seemed we should know more about our two friendly visitors. We checked our Encyclopedia Brittanica and as usual it tells us everything about everything except what we want to know. The E.B. tells us there are several kinds of bears, polar, grizzly, brown, black and the Malaysian small brownish black bear and that there aren't as many around as there used to be.

We put the Brittanica back in the dusty box and will keep it around until we get a chance to give it away or sell it. In our zeal to do our duty to our reading public we then went to the ultimate authority on bears and other wildlife, our own Poncho Roman of Cornucopia.

We learned that black bears don't quite hibernate in the true sense. In winter they crawl into a hole someplace and sleep deeply but can be aroused sometimes. Poncho doesn't recommend anyone trying to arouse a sleeping bear. The female bear sleeps separately from the male, although they snuggle up to keep warm.

After about seven or seven and a half months she gives birth to cubs weighing only about 12 ounces, pretty small for a 300-pound mother. The bear's body temperature and heart beat slow down a little but not like in true all-winter hibernation. Poncho says bears are pretty smart and recounts the time he and a friend were trailing a bear through the woods and watched his tracks in the light snow cover. After a while he stopped short and noticed the tracks were coming towards him instead of away. Poncho opined that the bear must have SUB TRACTED.

Our own bear still pays us regular visits down Blueberry Lane and then wanders into town. Bud Wenberg lives in the Heart of the Loop district here in Corny and has had his bird feeders ripped apart several times. Marg Gerstenberger watches him rest in a tree in back of her house where he stops on his way into town. He is seen around Ruth and George's Village Inn but he doesn't get into much trouble there, probably because the food is so good the patrons eat up everything served and don't leave much for bear hand outs. The bear's walk is fairly slow and clumsily graceful, but we don't think we want to try and out run him. These are the BEAR FACTS.

Rodrill Hukenlien dropped us a note saying he was very happy to read in the Letters to the Editor column of last week's paper, a message from a Phil O'Sopher from somewhere in Minnesota that his biography as recounted in our Bayfield-Washburn-Iron River-Press-Times-Pioneer is much appreciated. He told us he is bringing to our office two bottles of his famous Bark Point Elixir of Bliss for Mr. O'Sopher, compliments of Rodrill and Remingchester. He also told us not to worry about the labels on the bottles, one says "Lydia Pinkham's Compound" and the other "Watson's Vanilla Extract"...20 percent alcohol. He wants Phil O' to know that his spirits are stronger than that.

Mother-To-Be-Mallard

The big ones are coming back! We hear about the nice size trout being caught off Long Island and other spots out of Bayfield and Washburn and we believe the stories, too, but we personally have seen some dandies here in Corny. Joe Johnson and Al Jolson (sic) brought in a 14-pounder along with several other biggies. We may never have a big commercial fishing industry again, but it looks like we're headed for a healthy trolling industry.

Cornucopia's 25th annual Fish Fry is progressing on schedule. Ewald Heinonen has the many pounds of fish arranged for Vince Vander Venter, who has his waiters crew lined up and Gus Erickson has his fry cooks at the ready. Harold Ehlers has discussed the weather with the Lutheran minister and together they have conferred with someone who controls such things and reports a nice sunny day is in prospect. And Emmett Meagher over at the Sandpiper says he won't mind, too much, if all his faithful customers eat at the fish fry Sunday but he hopes they at least drop by for a cup of coffee and some fresh apple pie.

Mystery is Solved

We know our column is being read, by five people at least. That's how many called to explain how Floyd Loken's "Pijack" was named, and as expected the cruiser was christened, in honor of his owner's six daughters, Pat, Isabelle, Jackie, Anne, Cindy and Katherine. It could just as well have been the Cakjip." (Or, how about the "Kipjac" or Jikcap" or "Ackpij" or "Jackpi" or "Picjak" or...?)

MORTY SEZ: Some people have a heart of gold, but so does a hard boiled egg.

Old Mommy Nature

When Mother Nature provides something in abundance it seems to lose its value and in the case of flowers, seems to detract from their beauty and desirability. Orchids from Hawaii tend to be a nuisance. Crabgrass is generally a problem but in my lawn it would be a welcome addition to the scattered ferns and thimbleberry plants.

NOTES FROM THE HORN

Every field between Corny and Bayfield this time of year is exploding with buttercups and Indian paint brush (an orange colored daisy-like gem) by the millions, and we drive right by without noticing. Even our neighbor, a nature lover extraordinaire by the name of O'Leary is trying to get them off of his estate so the unobtrusive blade of grass will not become contaminated.

Our publisher stopped to view the scene on 13 and visited the harbor to check on operations of the U.S. government dredge working on the breakwater. He'll do a fine job of reporting, too, getting in the five "W's" and the "H" but like all city reporters visiting the hinterlands I'll bet he'll overlook the most important part. The Corps of Engineers, who are in charge, usually go about their business with dispatch and cool efficiency and sometimes with not too much regard for local problems and ecology. This group headed by the tug "Duluth," took time to carefully maneuver the dredge and equipment around the homestead of a much perturbed mother-to-be mallard who is still sitting on 12 lovely eggs.

Her nest is atop the breakwater, partially hidden in the rocks holding down the structure and without the Engineers' sympathetic understanding would have been destroyed. We thank the Corps for their feelings and efforts on behalf of motherhood, our local ecology and the purchasers of next fall's duck hunting stamp.

That personable, peripatetic proseman Professor Pulpwood stopped after visiting friends in Helsinki and Herbster. He says, sadly, that no one will remember his newspaper career in Bayfield and he's probably right, but he promises to prepare some items for this column sometime soon.

Mr. Ehlers... Mr. Cornucopia

Around the turn of the century Cornucopia was the scene of much activity, with the lumber industry buying, selling, cutting and burning all over the place. The fishing and farming industries were just getting started and about the best thing that happened in Cornucopia in 1908 was the arrival of a new employee, a bookkeeper, for the Flieth-Thompson Lumber Co. At age 15, Herman J. Ehler's impact on the community was probably not too noticeable but after the Lumber Company was dissolved and Herman came back to Corny as a partner in the Flieth-Ehlers Mercantile Co. nothing much has happened here that wasn't effected in some way by Mr. Ehler's presence.

Newsprint limitations won't allow a detailed history of Mr. Ehler's effort on behalf of the people and businesses in Cornucopia and columns could be written about his activities in the dairy, fishing, lumber and farming industries. Cornucopia was shaped by many people from all corners of Europe and America but one man stands out as a community maker.

Mr. Herman Ehlers — and even people his age or older still call him Mr. Ehlers — was born in Spencer, Wis. in 1893, moved to Corny in 1908, married Esther Johnson of Grandview in 1915 and acquired sole ownership of the Flieth-Ehlers enterprise in 1920. Mr. and Mrs. Ehlers had seven children. Three sons and one daughter are still with us, and son Harold has now taken over the operation of the family store.

Both Esther and Herman now reside in Ashland at the Court Manor.

Mr. Ehlers is dignity personified, a gentleman, and that word describes him better than any other, and has been part of our lives for better than a half century. Mr. Ehlers...Mr. Cornucopia.

Rabbit in Such a Dog Race

And now here is Rodrill Hukenlien again, this time with a new and outrageous proposition. Rodrill has heard all summer about the many celebrations in our area sponsored by every community boasting more than 100 residents. Each celebration features a "Run" or "Marathon" of some kind and Rodrill has decided to put on one of his own. Before he started on his spiel we said "NO," we wouldn't sponsor, promote nor even write about it in this column, having had some previous experiences with his proposals, but this new idea of his was so far out we couldn't resist telling our readers about it.

Hukenlien wants to start his "Run," to be called the "Hukenliener," at Albo's Vista del Lago Bar and Grill in Herbster, which is a logical place to start anything, and finish 10-feet out in Lake Superior past Chester Trost's place at the end of Bark Point. Thus far, the plan isn't too much different than any other race but this one features a "Catch the Game Warden" theme. Rodrill will charge each entrant 10 bucks to enter and will furnish each entrant with a sling shot and a supply of small Bark Bay stones to pepper the game warden with as he leads the pack out Bark Point Road with only a 50-yard head start. Rodrill promises to deduct $1 from each entry fee for each sling shot hit that produces a good yelp from the warden.

Our first question, of course, was which game warden would agree to be the rabbit in such a dog race. No problem, says Rodrill. We'll promise to tip off the warden with the names of those out-of-town sportsmen to whom he sells out-of-season deer meat and Lake Trout and the game warden can then arrest them and get credit for it and also maybe get a gold star and two Brownie points on his record. We had to agree that the people who buy such merchandise deserve to be caught and punished even though we occasionally support Rodrill Hukenlien in some of his other minor violations.

We told Rodrill we'd give his idea some thought as we are also getting a little bored with the conventional 10K and 2M "Runs" and thought this one would be unusual, particularly at the finish line 10 feet out in Lake Superior at Bark Point. We agreed to ask master photographer Chick Sheridan to be present and take pictures of the game warden as he is finally caught and perhaps also to take a picture or two of the winning racer. We'll donate a "HUKENLIENER" tee shirt!

The Affluent Society By-passes Corny

In Cornucopia we stand on the corner of Superior and Birch streets and visually locate practically every building in town, so street signs aren't as important as they are in metropolitan centers.

A native of Bayfield can direct another native with "Two blocks up from the old Tug Wilson home on Swede hill," or "One block west of the church on Catholic Hill," (or if both are real old timers, "Near the Island View Hotel)."

Most visitors, however, are used to street signs like Bayfield had all over town not too many years ago. These were easily read and quite attractive, and even the natives used them occasionally. We wonder where most of the signs went, and how do people find their ways nowadays.

Generosity

Corny's fine new boat launching ramp and black top parking has a nice little box suggesting that grateful boat owners drop an unspecified amount for maintenance. Human nature being what it is, donations have been somewhat less than expected. The first week netted $1.05. Decoration day weekend $3.50. Last week things were the best yet, over $12.50 was collected, an average of about 17 cents per boat launching. The Affluent Society evidently by-passes Corny, or maybe it's because they know no one is watching.

Morty just stopped in five minutes ago and gave instructions to cancel the last MORTY SEZ, and offered a new original...MORTY SEZ: "If I'm to be operated on I prefer a doctor without whiskers because they could get into the incision and cause me trouble."

According to the Chief

Chief Benny Parker, former Bayfielder and Coast Guard executive, stopped in to renew old acquaintances and discuss the merits and demerits of the proposed Apostle Islands National Park. Regardless of one's feelings it's worth listening to Benny as very few people know the islands as well as the chief.

People who like to eat out should appreciate the opportunities in our immediate area. Without mentioning names as the *Press* prefers to sell advertising rather than give it away, there are three excellent places in Bayfield, two more of the best in Corny, one each in Herbster and Port Wing, not to mention Madeline Island. Some larger towns only 12 miles away, again not mentioning any names, can't offer nearly as much. Per capita we probably do 10 times as well as world famous San Francisco.

Swim — Swam — Swum

Nature, not the politicians, decree that Bayfield should not be as Salmo, Cornucopia, Sand Bay and other such deltas. Unfortunately, most of them are privately controlled except our fine one at Corny which welcomes all non-littering citizens to enjoy it.

We can remember when beaches were for girls and very small boys only, and real swimmers headed for the city dock and preferred to spend the summer days diving for nickels and dimes and even pennies when things were tough.

"Throw in a nickel, throw in a dime, throw in a quarter all the time" was heard the length of the pier whenever the Madeline ferry came in. Ozzie and Morty Baldwin were the champs but all of us old timers can remember bringing home 40 or 50 cents on a good day. Someone should dredge the area between city dock and Henry Johnson's fish dock. He'd get a basketful of Indian Head pennies, Liberty nickels and maybe one of the 1913 variety worth thousands.

And this was when Bayfield was almost twice its present size and B.P.C. (before pollution control).

We don't know how large an aircraft our Cornucopia airport will handle but a sleek two-motored Beachcraft Baron made a perfect landing the other day using slightly over one-half of the field. We not only are Wisconsin's northernmost post office but have its northernmost airport, and a darn good one, too.

Jim O'Leary's summer home on Island View Drive in Squaw Point is pretty heavily wooded but he isn't satisfied and has filled in the few vacant spots with a planting of some 250 white pine seedlings. Anyone who dares to break off so much as a willow branch risks a good lashing from the sharp O'Leary tongue.

Visitors include an old friend and former Bayfield resident,

Professor Pulpwood, who expects to stay in Corny all summer. Oldtimers may remember the professor and his column in the *Bayfield Press* in the 1930s and with luck we may persuade him to take over the Scene for a time or two.

The Ice is Still Plenty Thick

Bobbing through the ice has always been a favorite winter sport in the Lake Superior waters off Port Wing, Herbster and Cornucopia. So far in 1978 it has been nothing but frustration. The northerly winds broke up the early ice and kept piling it up on top of itself all along the shoreline for a mile or more out into the lake. It's plenty thick enough to walk on or even to drive a car on but a bulldozer would be needed to make a path for a snowmobile.

A few hardy souls have trekked out a ways and dug some holes and after 20 inches or so of solid ice finally hit water, only to find another layer of ice under the water. Another ardent hole digger drilled a hole with his power auger and soon ran out of drill bit length at about 36 inches and finally gave up. He had tried to drill through a small iceberg which was stuck vertically in the surface ice.

For some suggestions we naturally called on our fishing expert from Oulu, Rodrill Hukenlien, and as usual we found him working on fishing equipment. This time he said he was tying flies. It looked to us like he was tying short lengths of fine line onto the top edge of a 100-foot net, spaced about 10 feet apart. He insisted he was fly tying and pointed out that he would tie a plastic fly on the end of the short piece of line and hang them all over one side of the net. This would attract the fish who would try to bite the fly and of course get himself caught by the gills in the process. We asked how he could consider this fly tying, and believe it or not he had an answer.

"We take along a pint of blackberry brandy and tie on a good one and when we see a game warden come along we fly all right, fast!"

We wonder how many comments we'll get on a typographical error in last week's column. We know very well that William the Conqueror beat Harold The Saxon in the year 1066 and not 1606 as printed. We had gunpowder by the year 1606. We still like the poem about 1978 when Bayfield beat Washburn two games straight.

The Scene on 13

Rodrill Hukenlien, Oulu's fishing expert, blew into town this week on the back of a pulp truck and presented us with his latest advice on bobbing for trout on Lake Superior. The fishing has dropped off the last week or so, not because of lack of ice or lack of fish, there is plenty of both, but under the heavy snow cover and on top of the three feet of ice is a nice layer of water.

This makes for very tough walking and snowmobiling and also very wet sitting while waiting for the fish to bite. It is Rodrill's opinion that this layer of water should be attractive to smelt as they could then find a fisherman's hole, swim into this water layer and make their way to the streams for spawning without being eaten by hungry lake trout. He suggests a snow shovel instead of a dip net to harvest the smelt and this would provide a three or four week advantage over the hoards of smelters who will invade us around the middle of April.

There are a lot of nice things about Spring, one of which is that we won't see so many cars with ski racks on top. These all look like police patrol cars until it is too late not to slow down to the double nickel. (55 miles per hour to those of you without C.B's).

There are many variations of Parkinson's Law, one of them being "When things are going well expect something to explode, corrode, erode, collapse, or disappear." Another is "When things can't get any worse you will be proven wrong." And there must be a dozen others.

Hale O'Malley:
The
Later Columns

Washburn People Do Come Home

Roger says: "Except for implying that Bill Bloomer hunkered you out of two trolling poles when in fact you've worked him for a lot of free fishing with those same poles, your Notes last week were O.K. Do another column, I'm busy."

He sure must be. Rueuben Daubner says, "You can catch Roger in the office now and then but mostly he just comes by to change signs."

Reuben is right. Here are some of the signs he hangs on the screen door, and I'm not making these up:
- "At George's Village Inn, one block West."
- "At Poncho's first door North."
- "Showing some nice people some nice property."
- "Out to Lunch (A long one on Sunday)."
- "Call O'Malley, 742-3304."
- "We'll be back about...(followed by a list of hours with an arrow pointing to one which for all you know may prove out)."

To be honest, I used that system myself when I was manning this office alone 20 years ago, and well remember once setting the arrow at 1 o'clock, coming back to reset it at 2:30, back again at 3 o'clock to set it for 4 o'clock, and finding a note from St. Paul friend, Tom George, "I don't care if you never come back."

Well, you really can do business with this office but you have to play your cards right. Patience and understanding, that's the answer. High pressure tactics will get you nowhere.

Never mind our frustrating signs. Do this please: Drive six miles west from Cornucopia toward Herbster. On your left see, neatly carved on wood, "Leather Galore." Go up that road a mile or so (it takes you past the Herbster Cemetery and some handsome homes that'll surprise you) and turn in at the word "Leather" on a pine tree. There meet a very interesting gal named Yvette Fleming, wife of Jim Fleming, who'll show you her basement shop where she works top grain leather into purses, belts, sandals, billfolds or just about anything you have in mind. A most gracious lady, and an artist.

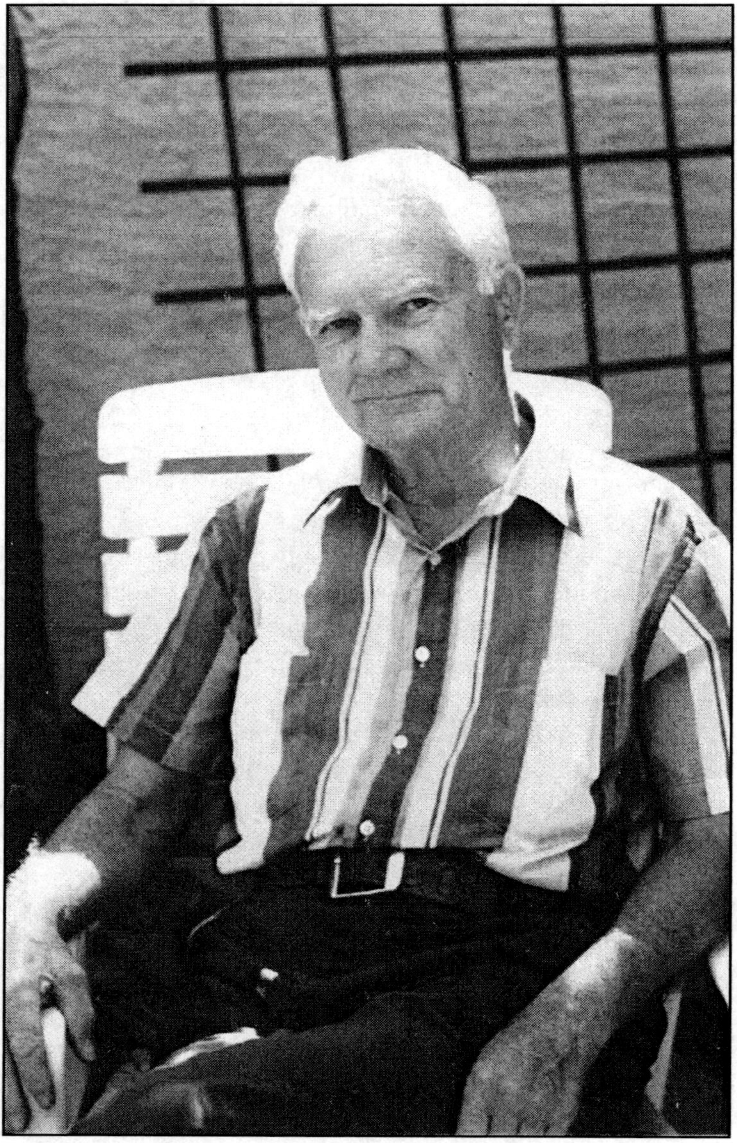

For $15.95 she made me a beautiful belt that I know for sure will last me at least two lifetimes. It has to. I'm just recovering from Marion's class reunion at the Homecoming — boy, Washburn people do come home — and feel like I've lived at least one-and-a-half already.

Never Trust an Editor

I've been sending theses notes into *The County Journal* too fast. Had the idea I'd get one or two columns ahead to cover the time we'll be traveling to Arizona, but they run two at once, darn them. Edna Buchanan, famous police reporter from the *Miami Herald* (she covers Miami Murders, lots of them) says, "Never trust an editor!"

I gave Bill Nolachek's grandson, Jake, age 10, a trout lure the other day and darned if he didn't try it out in the marine slip in Cornie and catch a 28-inch northern with it. Couldn't wait to tell me about it. Now I hope he gets a trout with it and I bet he will. He's a fisherman.

My suggestions to our editors that contributors from Bayfield, Washburn, Grand View, south have their photos over their columns never took root. Not only that, but they quit printing mine. They still run Darrell's though, beard and all. See Buchanan above.

We had a whole summer's worth of lightning at Bark Bay the other night, with high wind and heavy rain; I suppose you did too. Blew son, Scott's tent down with him in it; he clawed his way out and spent the rest of the night on our trailer's davenport, too short for him, but at least dry. Marion got no sleep. Scott was snoring, you were snoring, the cat was on the roof crying but wouldn't come in because there was a stranger in the house. What a night!

Days are still warm, in fact, these August days are the warmest we've had I think, and if Red and I and the Driftaway are going to bring in many more trout we'd better move.

Hey! He just called. "Days are getting short, we'd better get out there," so out we go.

Later: Got two nice lakers, and in the lunch Marion had packed for me I found this note: "I don't care if you don't catch a fish, I love you anyway."

Who needs fish?

Have things changed? You bet your laughing blue eyes they have. I can tick off a dozen marinas, all doing business and some with waiting lists, between Port Wing and around the peninsula to Ashland and La Pointe, must be well over 2,000 boats. Cornie, alone has 80 in the marina, all born in the last 30 years. Jim and Marge Miller opened Bayfield's in 1970; I was one of their first customers.

Of course, as in all marinas, most boats just sit there soaking up money while their owners are uptown spending what little they have left. My excellent Webster's New Collegiate Dictionary published 1951, only 39 years ago, doesn't even have the word marina in it.

It's a wonderful world. I want to live to 100 just to see what happens next, though in Al Gore's book, *Earth In The Balance*, which I'm struggling through, we'll all be wafted away by polluted rivers, gasping unbreathable air while being scoured by acid rain long before that. I hope I can finish his book before he finishes us but it looks like a close race.

Our Lake Superior sea gulls, herring gulls if you're an ornithologist, don't seem to be as sharp, or maybe as hungry as they used to be. Was a time when they'd snake a dead fish out of the water or off the beach before the next wave came, but I put the remains of a fresh-caught trout at water's edge the other night and it was a day-and-half before they found it. Finally, one, then a dozen, spotted it, dropped down and picked it clean. Really clean.

The Power of the Press

We're just back from a quiet New Year's in Mexico — Ron Roman calls New Year's Eve Amateur Night, and I quit competing several years ago, and what do I see in a recent *County Journal* but a big headline, "Washburn Dumps Bayfield 92-20."

Rats. Will we ever beat those guys?

Life can be cruel to be sure.

Retired geologist Gwen Schultz of Madison, who I think still owns a big lakeshore lot on Roman Point (just checked the plat book, she does), says I have to keep up my Glacial Kettle campaign. She's afraid that whole area will soon be overrun with condominiums and vacation homes. Well, not quite, but for sure those deep pits, the glacier formed thousands of years ago, are a neglected attraction and should be kept as they are. We just have to let our visitors know where they are and how to get there.

By way of picking up the torch (hard to keep a torch burning in glacier country in January). I've written old friend, Gary Connell, a director of the newly formed Bayfield Regional Conservancy, which I joined, that he might bring the members out there for a tour. Jim Miller says he'll guide them. No word yet; I'll let you know.

This interesting letter from Phil Mace, of both Washburn and Las Cruces, New Mexico just came in: "Dear Mr. O'Malley, You have probably heard this from many by this time, but, just for the record; the author of Archie the Cockroach stories, mentioned in your September 23 column, is Don Marquis.

Enclosed is a photocopy of the title page and part of the dust cover of my copy of the archy omnibus.

They are delightful stories that are not the least dimmed by time. Best regards. Phil Mackie"

Of course. When I wrote "Don Herald" I knew it didn't sound right, but now knowing I have a reader as astute as Mr. Mackie, whom I hope to meet sometime, I feel I've been given a boost. After this I'll be more careful about trusting my memory, which never was much. (I can recite "Trouble in River City" and "Casey

NOTES FROM THE HORN

at the Bat" though, word for word without missing a beat, and if you insist will add the Gettysburg Address.

Just talked with Dena Gibbs, and Steve Tower of Herbster's Cranberry Inn; they aren't Italian but serve great Italian dinners and right now are hoping they'll get enough snow to bring in the snowmobilers. Been a problem. "We have about three inches right now," Dena said. "I can see the tip of the the grass from our front window. Send some snow!" I said I would, and I bet as you're reading this it's snowing right now.

The Power of the press.

Press On More Doorbells

So our faithful Editor Darrell Pendergrass finally got his buck! I admire his persistence, and hope his patient wife, Queenie, likes venison. Hate to think of Darrell, with all he has to do putting out this paper, having to eat a whole deer all by himself, not that I doubt for a moment he'd do it.

I think this is the place to quote the fellow — can't think of his name — who started that worldwide chain of McDonald's Hamburgers:

Press On

"Nothing in the world can take the place of persistence. Talent will not; nothing is more common than unsuccessful men with talent. Genius will not; unrewarded genius is almost a proverb. Education will not; the world is full of educated derelicts. Persistence and Determination alone are omnipotent."

As a former life insurance salesman (but nobody wants to be a salesman, we were "Field Representatives" or "Estate Planners." Good grief) who has probably rapped on more doors, pressed more doorbells hoping nobody was home and barged into more offices, uninvited, than any man living, I swear by that statement.

No buck or doe has anything to fear from me though. I like to see them alive and pretty much view hunters (though I have some good friends there) as the deer does.

I once, in Mexico, shot a dying dog, had to do it but sure didn't like it and feel bad about it yet, and over the years have had to shoot a few cats including one tough old tom who was determined to kill our pet cat "Beargrease," a born slob. Marion insisted I do something about that devil, who at the moment was sitting on the beach at the corner of our trailer, giving me a look that plainly said, "Well? What about it?" So I shot him. Hated it, and went in the house and told Beargrease, "I've just shot a better man then you'll ever be!" and felt a little better.

Let's get off this subject before I lose the few hunting friends I have.

NOTES FROM THE HORN

I've just re-read the story of the new ferryboat purchase by the Madeline Island Line in Burlington, Vt., and brought through the New York Canal System as far as Toledo, Ohio, where she'll be berthed until they run her the rest of the way to Bayfield next spring.

I envy those guys, Mike Radtke, Bob Divine, Phil Peterson and the three crew members from Lake Champlain, guiding a 43-foot cumbersome craft like this through 46 locks, some just 44 feet wide. That took some doing. With Jim Miller, and later Marion, I've run the Erie Canal, called the New York Barge Canal at the time, twice, once with the *Cat's Paw*, then the *Lida Rose*, each only an eight-foot beam. No big thing, still a challenge.

Those guys have something to brag about.

I'm glad to see Jeff Orthman with his "Merry Mumble" column is back. I know how he felt losing his dog, Boone, but glad he has a new pup, Sam. Nothing like catching a new pup chewing up your shoe to take your mind off your troubles. Your other troubles.

The new group, the Bayfield Regional Conservancy to which of course I've signed on, sounds like it's really going to do something. I've just written Gary Connell, one of the directors, that I hoped they'd join my Glacial Kettle campaign as a tourism promotion. Also asked Jim Miller to guide them out there. That natural phenomenon, six miles south of Cornie and just off County C, has been there some 10,000 years but nobody knows about it.

See paragraph three. They will.

Snakes Masquerading as Fish

Boy, good thing I've never tried to make a living as a reporter. Last week I wrote of seeing a couple bicycling into Cornie, the man towing a baby strapped into a homemade two-wheeled cart. Turned out to be John and Lynda Nedden Durst of Lost Creek's Mosquito Farm. I wrote they were towing their year-old baby girl, Jennifer. Trouble is, as John politely explained to me at the Land Use Sub-Committee meeting last night, the baby is a boy, born July 10, 1997. Name is Dylan. Age two, not one.

Too late to stop the press. Fortunately Darrell doesn't pay me enough to make me worth firing.

Bob Kubec suggested I attend this Land Use meeting since they had on the agenda the changing of the name "Jodi Road" to "Glacial Kettle Road" which, of course, I was all for. Committee members there were with Chairman Bradley Schultz, Scott Griffith, Kellie Pederson, John Johanning and John Nedden-Durst. Also young Dylan, who approved of everything.

I, of course, was an innocent bystander, but got the impression the name change to Glacial Kettle Road may actually happen. Great to have some backing, and heartening to see people here really care what happens to their home country.

We'll be O.K.

It always troubles me to see a bird I can't identify, which is most of the time. I'm safe on seagulls, robins, crows and bald eagles but from there on, no. Now I've just spotted a little bush-hopper I'm pretty sure is a chickadee. I'm long on chickadees but you don't see chickadees in summer, do you? They're Fall and Winter birds. Aren't they?

Rats. Birdwise, I'll never amount to anything.

Had a nice talk yesterday with Washburn Librarian Cheryl Michalski, who will help you find the book you want if she has to scour the country. Right now I'm seeking information on the Keweenaw Peninsula which Red Anderson and I want to circle in the Driftway this summer. If our respective ladies, Blades and

Barb, don't talk us out of it. Or we don't chicken out on our own.

On birds again: a small duck, a hooded merganser (I looked her up) has again this summer been parading a family in Bark Bay; started with eight, a couple of them sometimes astride her back. They paddle along at a good clip, heads often in the water studying the bottom; if one finds himself falling behind he actually runs on the water to catch up. Every now and then they dive and disappear for a minute, then pop up like corks. Then the other day there were only five, and this morning two!

I know what's happened they're diving in the weedbed where the big northern pike hang out, very dangerous territory for ducklings. I've never really cottoned to northerns, though over the years I've caught my share of them. A long, slim, mean-looking thing with an undershot jaw that reminds me of the late Sara Delano Roosevelt. They're snapping up our cute little mergansers, I think they are.

Drat their slimy, scaly hides. I say they're snakes masquerading as fish.

Never let the Flag Touch the Ground!

Were you taught as a kid that you must never let the flag touch the ground? I was and it still holds. I've just replaced our old balsam flagpole here on the lake and hoisted a new flag bought at Ungrodt's for $10, a bargain. Balsam trunks are always straight as an arrow, light and easy to lift up, the trick is to find one on the beach already peeled and dried. You could cut one green but they're full of pitch and of course you have to trim the branches flush with the trunk or the flag catches on the stumps.

So we have a new flag, a beauty, and I'm as proud of it as though I were Francis Scott Key himself, and first cousin to Betsy Ross. It hasn't touched the ground either, and won't.

Marina. Cornie has a dandy, and I have a good dictionary published in 1951 in which the word marina doesn't even appear. That's how fast our world has changed. I'm loyal to this old *Webster's New Collegiate* though, it's the only one I've seen that tells you what the zero on the Fahrenheit scale stands for. All right, water freezes at 32 degrees, boils at 212 degrees doesn't it? And we say, "It was 20 below zero of course. So what does the zero stand for? Ah. "The zero point represents the temperature produced by mixing equal quantities, by weight, of snow and common salt."

Now I know why my mother packed rock salt and snow in the freezer being a wooden bucket in which four paddles turned inside a big metal container holding what would be, frozen, her delicious strawberry or raspberry or peach sherbet. The snow and salt combination brought the temperature down, I presume, to Dr. Fahrenheit's zero. I can taste the sherbet yet, and when I got my first job as a clerk in Ole Holm's drugstore I saved up $4 and bought my mother a new freezer. The ladies of her Tuesday Club thought that was hilarious.

When I started this column it was a muggy 78, the winds just switched to the north and it's suddenly 67. If this keeps up we'll be testing that Fahrenheit zero. Well not quite, its still August.

Stinkpotters they Call Us! May 11, 2000

Letter just in from Washburn's Gary Holman, who says, "You won't need any reminders of the Washburn Homecoming I'm sure, however, many Washburn musicians who have played in my Washburn band, high school or city, are being recruited for a reincarnation of the Washburn City Band and they will be informed of this opportunity."

Flattered, I of course immediately answered, "I should know better but count me in." Well why not? He added, "Thoughts of macerated lips, blistered feet, weakened knees, fuzzy vision or reduced blood supply should be no reason to avoid participation in this noble cause."

Gary didn't specifically refer to being in their parade, but I'm afraid that's the plan. I was in the last one five years ago, walked — and played — a mile in a cold drizzle and barely made it. I was 80 and now at 85, well, I don't know. On that march five years ago I remember seeing the sign Bratley Funeral Home up ahead and thinking if I could make it past that without becoming a customer, I'd be O.K. I did, but it was a near thing.

Gary's letter really takes me back, way back to 1946, when, having personally won World War II as a cook in the Merchant Marines, I came home to Bayfield — had a wife, two kids and no job. Also had a trumpet and Washburn had a City Band that practiced every Thursday night; so one night I showed up and took a seat, uninvited, in the trumpet section.

Nobody told me I was lousy; wasn't necessary. I not only couldn't play for sour apples but when they stuck a simple march in 6/8 time in front of me, couldn't even read what I couldn't play.

I remember most of those fellows, gentlemen all: "Kid" Wedin and Billy Anderson, trombones, (Billy could have played trombone anywhere); "Flutta" Ungrodt, French horn, a kid with an Irish name, I think Monahan, who could really play trumpet; and band leader George Bergman, who'd drop the baton and grab his clarinet once in awhile. Oh, Ernie Holman, too, who played really fine trumpet. A few others — they'll come to me.

I'll always remember George Bergman, a man I came to love. It just wasn't in him to deliberately kick someone out of the band, but one day when I parked my '31 Chevy in front of his store he came out, leaned in the window with one foot on the running board and we talked a little. I could see his struggle. "Of course our fellows are old-timers, Hale," he said. "I know it's really hard, when you haven't had the basic training, to hold your own with them. I know how difficult it is..." and so on, doing his best not to say what we both knew perfectly well why, "...If you feel you should drop out, Hale, we'll understand."

I couldn't let the poor man suffer any longer so said, "That's right, George; well, see you Thursday night!" I knew what his short, choked response would be. So do you, but never mind. This is a family paper.

I never did get very good on the horn, haven't yet, but in time at least wasn't a total disgrace to the Washburn band, and as the weeks rolled along George and I became good friends. He actually came to like me and once told me so. That was 50 years ago and you can bet I haven't forgotten.

Sometime later I moved to St. Paul, working for the Guardian Life Insurance Company, and joined the 3M band there the same way I'd joined Washburn's. But I could at least carry my weight now, and once on a trip home, trumpet in hand, I rang George Bergman's bell.

"I'm here for my lesson."

"You're two years late!"

He set out some music and we played a duet which I taped; not very good, and not much for sale.

So yes, Gary, count me in. I can't let George Bergman down. Or you, either.

An entertaining story on Darrell's Brule River trout fishing took up a full page in a recent issue here, complete with photos, one of them a six-inch rainbow, the sole catch of the day.

I don't believe his partner, Dangerous Dan Bloomquist, really made all the nasty remarks about fishing with worms Darrell attributed to him, though. If he did — well, never mind, never mind.

I never understood this idea that fly fishing is the only acceptable way to catch a trout, that fishing with worms for bait is simply not done, not in polite society. It's the same with sailboat people, some of them anyway, have toward power boats. "Stinkpotters" they call us, though they all have Yamaha auxiliary engines they crank up when they really have to get someplace.

Anyway, that six-inch rainbow, which in the closeup shot of him looks more like what we used to call Sebago Salmon, was apparently the only fish caught all day, and of course, they released him. I hope Darrell catches him two or three years from now when he'll weigh at least five pounds. Catches him on a worm and makes Dangerous Dan take his picture.

Of course I like seeing my picture heading this column and still hope to see shots of our other stringers. I read them all, including the regulars like Eric Sharp and Brent Fuqua whose photos do appear. By the way they write I feel I know those fellows, and in their head shots they look the way you expect them to. I'm sure Velma Volk, Virginia Wallin and the others would too, but I'd like to see their pictures just to be sure.

Lemon or Lyme Disease

With winter coming on I think I'll soon have to call this column "Notes To" instead of Notes From the Horn. Just got a call from Washburn girl, Ruth Peterson, once Ruth Bodin, inviting us to a Washburn dinner party at the Beefeaters Restaurant here in Phoenix, Nov. 9. Expected attendees, so far, are: Chet Sanger, Eldy Robinson, Joe Homan, Bob Spears and daughter, Karen, of course Ruth herself, and the former Marion Corning of Washburn, now Mrs. Hale O'Malley; Mr. O'Malley himself, born and raised in Bayfield, to be admitted as a Washburn in-law.

Others not yet heard from will show, I'm sure, then as the days shorten we'll see more, from Bayfield maybe Jim and Marge Miller, Bob and Dona Hadland, Jim and Jean Stenberg, possibly even Wally and Dorothy Nordin, plus some citizens from Cornie, Herbster and Port Wing. But we don't want to denude the whole South Shore, I'm sure they'll leave an armed guard.

Now another nice letter from Cornucopia Postmaster Chis Fiege with two dozen more old snapshots of Bayfield people I knew 50, 60 and 70 years ago.

I spent the whole morning trying to identify them, got quite a few, agonized over the ones I was sure I recognized but couldn't name , and collapsed, exhausted.

I thought when you reached your 80s life got easier. It doesn't. Read on.

Almost everybody from the East, and when you're in Arizona two-thirds of the country is back east, sees us as the home of rattlesnakes, side-winders, centipedes, tarantulas, black widow spiders and scorpions and, of course, we are. But like that tiny Wisconsin tick that's supposed to give you the deadly Lyme Disease or Lemon Disease or whatever it is, you almost never see them.

Last week though, at our little place in Mexico, 200 miles south of Phoenix, Marion "Blades" O'Malley met a scorpion. Getting up at midnight she put her bare foot on one and got zapped on her big toe. The pain kept getting worse, "Never had anything hurt so much in my life," she says and at 2 a.m. I drove into the office of the Red Cross, always someone on duty there, and four well-trained Mexicans followed me to the house in an ambulance, lights flashing, gave her an intravenous shot and some liquid to prevent dehydration, loaded her on a stretcher and rushed her to the hospital. I could hardly keep up.

The doctor put her on a wooden board, dripped more liquid and pain-killer in her (which didn't seem to work) kept checking on her until 6 a.m., charged me $50, a bargain, and we drove home.

The Red Cross never once mentioned money but two days later, all this behind us, pain gone except for a little numbness in that toe, we left for Phoenix and I dropped off $100 on the way out, least I could do.

We're used to seeing their ambulance on the side of the highway as we leave with a fellow holding a can for donations; I've always dropped in a few coins but from now on I'll do better.

It'll be a pleasure.

Scorpion in Spanish, by the way, is alacran. Thought you'd like to know.

"Dear Mr. O'Malley:

Just read and enjoyed your column, again, as always. I loved your "Real Girl."

I wonder how many older women's memories were jogged by your "real girl."

I remember so well how it felt to be a "real girl," wearing the swishy skirt with the little belted waist. The high heels, that made us feel oh, so feminine. Sometimes a peasant blouse (that was always very girly).

And, yes, we appreciated you boys, who let us know, you appreciated us. You were not the "today's' cool."

Alas, many girls today, including my own darling daughters, have little patience for dresses and certainly not the wonderful feminine dresses of the '40s, '50s and even '60s.

As the song goes, "Those were the days my friend!" And yes–
"We thought they would never end."

"Well Mr. O'Malley, I certainly hope you will go on forever. Wishing you the very best of health, please keep those memories coming.

A faithful 63-year-old reader. (Would sign my name, I'm not being mysterious — just afraid I'll see it in print)."

Didn't Even Smoke Cigarettes

Chris Fiege, long-time efficient and well-liked Postmaster of Wisconsin's Northernmost Post Office at Cornucopia has just sent me two old snapshots taken about 75 years ago and asks if I can identify the people.

You bet your laughing blue eyes I can, Chris! One of those pictures was taken at your Grandfather Hank Fiege's house in Bayfield, a birthday party for someone. I know them as though they were here in the room with me and in 75 years they haven't aged a bit.

Harold "Dutch" and Josephine Stark; Hand and Agnes Fiege; Roy and Ellen Okerstrom; Johnny and Helen Sayles; "Butch" and Evelyn Lodle (Is Evelyn right? I'm not sure). Gus and - darn it I can't recall her first name either - Mrs. Weber; Doug and Middy Knight: Joe and Greta O'Malley; my folks, and I see my mother had just had her hair bobbed. In the early '20s the New Woman was breaking out all over the place and she wasn't going to be left behind.

The other shot was probably taken at the hunting shack on Siskiwit Lake, most of the same fellows, the Cochran Gang, and I recognize Doc Harris and his brother, George. Ed Bassett and, I think, John Anderson from the bank are there. (Doctor Harris lanced my hand, infected by a Fourth of July squeegee when I was about eight. It hurt).

Hank Fiege is in that picture, holding a bottle of his favorite drink, kummel, a kind of cordial flavored with caraway seeds (I looked it up), which nobody else drank.

Did I know them? My dad had sent me a print of that birthday party shot long ago; on the back he's written, "Did we ever have fun? Didn't even smoke cigarettes."

Of course not. Not many years before that men either smoked cigars or a pipe and women didn't smoke anything. Cigarettes were effeminate and, so I'm told, was wearing a wristwatch. Women wore ankle-length dresses and waist length hair usually gathered up in a bun, and if you were walking with a lady you walked on the curb side so she wouldn't get splattered with mud from the horses clumping by. That courtesy originated long before I came along but was still alive when I did, and I'm still not comfortable walking on the inside.

I think the Cochran Gang, and the Hell Divers in the next shack, did as much drinking and singing as they did hunting. I remember Dad telling me about the time he and Gus were rendering the Irving Berlin ballad, "A Russian Lullaby" a soothing waltz when properly sung but anything Gus sang came out like the William Tell Overture. "Gus! Gus!," Dad said, "This is a lullaby! This young Russian mother is rocking and softly singing her baby to sleep. She croons, "Hushabye my baby," she doesn't yell "Hush-A-Bye."

"Not in Russia!" Gus says.

Poncho Roman once told me, Same thing going on always did. Only different bunch doing it."

I suppose, but do we have as much fun? I wonder.

A Fridge Full of Bratwursts & Beans

"This north country can furnish enough weather in a 24-hour day to last a month" Ror a Labor Day Sunday, Red Anderson, Chuck Ludwigson and I planned a fishing trip. We would meet at the Cornucopia Marina at 1:30, take the *Driftaway* for an afternoon's trolling, get back in time for a Bark Bay brats-and-beans evening beach picnic with other old friends we would invite. All this weather permitting, of course.

Morning of the big day was murky, lake hidden in thick fog but the sun was trying to peak through. It might clear up. It didn't. By 11 a fine drizzle, 12 pouring rain, still raining when we met at the marina. Fog so dense you couldn't see fifty feet. The rain seemed to be easing up though. Should we go?

Of course, we'll go. With Hale O'Malley at the helm, old salt who, on Lake Superior, can tell exactly where he is by sticking his finger in the water, what's to worry?

We creep out of the harbor and poke into the fog, visibility zero, headed due north on the principle that all we'll have to do to get back is head due south. Rolling in the sea though, the compass doesn't hold still and besides that, the northeast wind keeps pushing the bow northwest to the left (pardon, to port) So, over-compensating, we keep swinging between northeast and northwest, now and then actually headed due north.

"Fish on!," Chuck, trolling with a dipsy-diver holding his lure down probably 20 feet, boats a nice trout. Red and I relax a little, after all when you have a guest aboard you don't want him going home skunked.

The fog never lifts, we are maybe two miles out, see nothing, have seen nothing but gray since we left port, but by 3:30, we have four fish in the boat. Nothing big enough and we head back. Now the wind pushes us to starboard. I keep pulling us back to port and sometimes south. Can't take time to stick my finger in the water and announce our exact location.

Never mind. Creeping along, one eye straight ahead, the other on the depth finder so as it gets shallower, we will know we are approaching land, which I hope will be sand beach instead of steep rocky bank. Suddenly, sure enough, trees, then beach. Nothing to it. We turn left (sorry, port) and in a few minutes, there's the Cornucopia Harbor, right where we left it.

To Bark Bay, a good beach bonfire, old friends Jim and Marge Miller, Terry and Shirley Welty, Joan Cook, Bob and Dona Hadland, Jean Ludwig, son, Marion O'Malley and three hungry fishermen all set for bratwurst and beans and what do we get? Another downpour. We tough it out for awhile, finally toss in the towel and drive to the Village Inn where Chuck, knowing this country, has thoughtfully made reservations for twelve. Great dinner, didn't even have to do the dishes. We ran to our cars in the rain.

The weather? I woke up at 3 a.m. and looked out the window. No wind, a perfectly clear sky with a million stars, fog long gone, absolutely beautiful, and there was the Big Dipper, low over the lake, looking like it could scoop up all of the Bark Bay with one swipe.

We have a fridge full of bratwurst and beans. "Plenty for twenty" as the old song says. Plus Joan's donated potato salad and huge cake and Jean's two pies (no room, she had to take those back). It will all keep for awhile and we will still have that picnic, weather permitting.

Birds 'Tern' Me On

Marion and I are just back from a short trip to our little place in Mexico, where we were attacked by terns.

Honest.

We were riding our little Honda ATC-90s down the beach to the estuary where we sometimes catch little silvery leatherjacks every cast and MOST of the time catch nothing, and found ourselves getting dive-bombed by a flock of terns. Terns are seafowl about half the size of herring gulls and they usually mind their own business which is diving for minnows.

Watching a hundred or so plunging straight down into a school of little fish reminds you of those war movies of kamikaze attacks; this time they were attacking us and they were pretty mad, too.

We couldn't figure it out. They'd circle over us about fifty feet up, peel off in a vertical dive at our heads and make a three-G pullout at the last second. Even though they dropped no bombs it was unnerving. We stopped and shut off our motors-and they immediately took off. We started up again and back they came; we stopped, turned off the machines and away they went again.

We finally got the message — they didn't like the sound of those little motors! Now if you can explain this, or even make a decent guess at it please write me at 2662 N. 43rd Avenue, Phoenix, Arizona 85009. In fact, please write even if you don't have a guess, we'd like to hear from you. Mail from home is always important and Arizona is great but Lake Superior is home!

Birds kind of took over this last trip, come to think of it. Did you ever see a partridge leading her chicks down a woodland path, the chicks all coming along in single file? Then if you startle the mother she scampers away, dragging a wing to make you think she's crippled, and while she's decoying you the chicks all grab a leaf and pull it over them.

Think I'm making this up? Nope, it's a fact, and if you doubt it you can ask Roger about it, we've both seen it and looked it up in the Burgess Bird Book to find out where the chicks went.

Marion and I just saw this same game on the desert in Mexico, this time with a family of gamble's quail and if there is anything in the world cuter than a partridge chick it's a little gambel's quail. They have a little topknot like a tiny marble bouncing above their heads and I think the only reason it's there is vanity, just vanity — they want to out-cute a partridge.

Mother quail spotted us and immediately scampered off over the sand making loud squawks of alarm, and the babies all dove into a desert bush. I walked over there and though the bush wasn't a foot high and three feet across and I knew they were in there. I couldn't see a thing or hear so much as a slight rustle. But I could hear mother a few dunes off squaking orders: "Keep Quiet! Don't Move! He's still there!" So I backed softly away, never wishing to be where I'm not wanted.

A couple of cactus wrens yelled at our cat Rip, but that's not news. Rip is scared of everything and besides, all wrens are even tempered — mad all the time.

An interesting trip, as it goes, and I'll say one thing — the next time we go down that beach I'm going to have a pocketful of pebbles. And I will leave, if necessary, no tern unstoned.

NOTES FROM THE HORN

Cancel My Subscription

Just back from two weeks in Mexico; got up early 5:30 to make sure we'd be early at the border. For 30 years we've been waved through: "U.S. citizens?" "Sure, what're you bringing from Mexico?" "Nothing" "O.K. Have a safe trip." But since September 11, you open your trunk; pop the hood and two uniformed guards poke through your luggage. This takes some time, and you could be inching along in a mile-long wait for two hours or more.

Crossing into Mexico is no problem, the Mexicans want that tourist dollar and wave you right through.

An interesting story by Barbara Brown Meredith in the Nov. 8 issue quotes Bob Mackreth, historian of our Apostle Islands National Lakeshore, on the changes over the years. From "The establishment of a thriving fur trading industry that lasted 200 years" through the brownstone quarrying, 1869 to 1897, then a "booming logging industry lasting until its collapse in the Great Depression, with the only viable industry left — tourism."

Funny thing about tourism. Its spoken of as "an industry without smokestacks," which is true enough if you think of it as a real industry like commercial fishing or logging or quarrying brownstone.

I guess it is. Look at our thriving marinas, practically touching each other all along the shore of the Bayfield Peninsula, at our motels, fine eating places and our snowmobile trails keeping you entertained year-round, all geared to serving our out-of-town visitors, without whom we're back to quarrying brownstone and people aren't buying brownstone anymore.

In the stack of junk mail and bills waiting for us was a *County Journal* clipping headed "Bayfield Area Active Sports Alliance tours Glacial Kettles" sent us by Fern (Mrs. Toby) Pedersen of Ashland. Fern is a Washburn classmate of Marion's and is one of those people who never forget you; she knew any mention of this natural phenomenon whose deep gouges in the earth have been waiting for 10,000 years for somebody to notice, would excite me.

As geologists reckon time 10,000 years is an eye blink. But there they are, and here we are, and if we want to give our visitors something extra to see here all we have to do is change the name Jodi Road to Glacial Kettle Road and put up signs leading you in; an easy 1.7 miles brings you to a big natural flat parking area, and you can drive right to the brink of the largest kettle (there are about 20), a cone-shaped gouge nearly 200 feet deep. One good man with a chainsaw could cut a nice walking path around the rim of it in a day.

Decent of reporter Eric to mention my kettle campaign, and reading his by-line; Eric Hjerstedt Sharp. I'm reminded I could never make it as a real reporter. A reporter has his facts and his spelling exactly right, or he gets a call the minute the paper hits the stands: "Hidgersted Sharp? I don't drive a green car with a black stripe! I drive a black car with a green stripe! Cancel my subscription!"

Ah, well, feeling as generous and forgiving as I do this morning I'm tempted to overlook Eric's failure to mention that while the kettles are indeed 12.5 miles from Washburn on County C, they're only six miles from Cornucopia.

Only tempted.

Catalysis

CATALYSIS: the causing or accelerating of a chemical change by the addition of a substance (catalyst) which is not permanently affected by the reaction.

A neighbor in our 148-unit townhouse complex has the real thing, a cat named Bosco, who as a half-grown kitten, walked into our patio a few weeks ago. Had a red collar so we knew he was someone's pet. Marion was about to tack a Lost Cat notice on the bulletin board when the owner, Marty Tauriainen, showed up and identified him.

I'd thought Marty a little stand-offish but we started talking cat; we both speak fluent cat. Bosco, he said, likes everybody; our cat, Kelly, kind of likes us but nobody else including all other cats. So while our pets had nothing in common, Marty, Marion and I did, and became friends right there.

Bosco stops by almost every day now, saunters into the house, checks out Kelly's dish while Kelly growls, occasionally uses the sandbox in the bathroom, and continues his rounds.

A catalyst. The real thing.

The great thing about the Police and Sheriff's Reports is the specialization — did the fellow locked in the post office a year or so ago ever get out? What happened to him anyway? Did the lady reporting a dead bear on the road do what she was advised: "Don't skin him. Load him in a truck and take him to a deep freeze?" If so, did she hoist him, unskinned, into her pickup by herself? Did she then find a big enough deep freeze? Is he still there? Doggone.

Did the problem drinker recently insulting lady customers in the Firehouse Bar and ordered out, who left making threatening remarks to the bartender ever return, or try to?

I suppose we'll never know. Fun thinking about it though, and these little mysteries really spice up the paper.

Short column this week. Long enough.

Cedar Boards Went To The Shingle Mill

Mell Clark, 85, born and brought up in Bayfield is writing a book about his home town and has just sent me a copy of Chapter 14:

The sawmill was the largest industry in Bayfield, employing many of the men in the area. It was started by Mr. Pike in the late 19th Century and was later owned by Mr. Wachsmuth. From our home we could see most of the mill buildings located below us in the millyard.

Most of the logs came to the mill by rail or boat. The railroad hauled the logs to the sawmill site. A tug boat and scow would bring in large loads of logs from the islands. Most of the logs were put in the mill pond and were later prepared for the mill. The scow or barge was a large wooden boat with a flat bottom. At one end was the steam engine and the operator's room. From his position, he could see the entire area.

A large swivel-mounted boom extended from his location to about mid-ship, where it was attached to a large clam, a machine which could grasp logs and move them. The operator, with various levers could lift and turn the clam, could open and close the jaws, and place the logs to any desired position. Several logs could be unloaded together into the water with this equipment. A number of large logs chained together, also called a boom, was placed near the mill pond to prevent the logs from floating away. The tug boat would then tow the empty scow back to the lumber camp on the island for a new load.

When the logs had soaked in the mill pond enough, they were prepared for the sawmill. This was done by two men, one on each end of a log. They were called skinners and wore special shoes with steel cleats for safety on the slippery logs and short pants to prevent getting wet. The tools they used to remove loose bark and knots were an adz, a cutting tool with a thin arched blade set at right angles to the handle, and a short pike pole, a wooden shaft with a pointed steel head. When the logs were ready, they were taken to the conveyor, which pulled the log up to the second floor where it was rolled on to a machine called a carriage, operated by steam.

The operator, the sawyer, sat near the front and worked the levers which adjusted the logs to receive the desired cut. The large endless steel band saw with large cutting teeth was located on the ground floor near its steam-driven engine. It passed over a wooden pulley then extended to a similar wooden pulley on the second floor, where it was lined up with carriage.

When the log was positioned for the cut, the carriage would be moved forward to bring the log in contact with the saw blade. When the log was cut, the carriage would return the log for the next cut. The sawyer's work required a lot of skill and was a dangerous operation. The boards cut from the logs were sent to smaller saws where the ends were trimmed to the desired length.

Cedar boards went to the shingle mill, where they were cut and shaped to make roof shingles, packed in a bundle called a square. The lath mill cut thin strips of wood used in building houses. The laths were fastened to the building studs to hold the plaster in place for the construction. The slab wood and trimmings were sold as firewood, sent to the burner, or used as fuel for the boilers.

The cut boards were inspected and separated according to quality. Those that were free of knots, splits, or cracks were sent to the planning mill for processing. This was a separate and noisy place where the boards were sent through a large lathe with sharp cutters to make a smooth finish on all four sides. The finished lumber was stacked up to air dry to be used in the building industry.

The curled-up shavings, called excelsior, were packed in containers and sold to companies for packaging. The saw dust picked up from the floor by a large vacuum and blower that was mounted on the roof. It was then blown outside through a large pipe into a huge pile. It was sold to fishermen who had ice houses and to farmers and builders for insulation and for keeping ice.

The constant usage of the band saw blade and the blades of the other saws made sharpening a necessity. The band saw was removed from its fastening, rolled up, and sent to the filing shop where there was equipment for that work. The dull blades or tools needing sharpening were clamped in a vise which held an item securely while being worked on. Long-handled mill files were used for sharpening. This was another kind of work that required a great deal of skill. The workmen were known as filers, a most desirable trade, which paid a high wage.

A tramway system, consisting of an elevated wood structure, extended the length of the millyard, including several docks or slips, as they were called. It was built to haul small cars loaded with lumber. The cars ran on small steel rails with suitable switches. The cars were loaded with rough green boards at the sawmill and pulled by a horse to the proper area. The lumber was then piled in crisscross fashion to air dry. The tramway was extended to the surrounding docks where the lumber could be stacked. Large lumber-carrying boats could load the lumber into their holds to take to the ports along the Great Lakes to supply the high demand for the wood for buildings and furniture.

We played with the tram cars when the mill was not operating. It was like a small railroad, great fun to push the cars, then ride for a short distance. I am sure that the workers did not mind looking for the cars when returning to work next day. One Sunday morning after Sunday School, Harry Hessing and I decided to check out the sawmill tram. It was very quiet at the mill, and we had it all to ourselves, or so it seemed.

We were switching the tracks on one of the rails when Harry fell and injured his arm. About this time, Mr. Egan, the watchman, appeared on the scene. Harry was crying and I was scared. We were afraid of the watchman. When he saw that we were all right, he said, "You boys get the hell out of here and don't come back again." Needless to say, that ended our fun on the tram.

One summer during school vacation it was decided to have a woodworking class for the boy's Sunday School class, Mr. Smith was designated to be the instructor. He was a young man who served as the church assistant in other activities. Our shop would be in the church kitchen. Our first class was a tour of the sawmill, very interesting and informative. When the tour was over, we were given some boards that could be used in our class. The pieces were smooth and easily cut with our class saws. We were taught how to cut and fit the parts of a birdhouse, and how to sand them and assemble them. They were later painted in different colors. This was a good project and we all learned a great deal about wood and its uses. We learned to build items by ourselves, and applied this training in Manual Training classes in school.

When the forest trees were cut and used in the area, there was no raw material for the mill. The Wachsmuth Saw Mill and Lumber Company shut down completely during the late summer of 1927. This was a devastating time for Bayfield, with the loss of work for so many. Our home on Fifth Street was on the bluff above the mill. From that vantage point on our front porch, we watched the closing of the sawmill as it began with the removal of the burner. This was a tall steel structure with a rounded dome covered with wire mesh to contain sparks and embers while allowing the smoke to pass through.

The base had several large doors to where the bark and slabs of unwanted wood scraps were burned. It was also used to supply some heat for the steam boilers. On the scheduled day, the dynamite, which had been placed in the base, was set off causing a tremendous noise. The huge burner toppled and crashed to the ground. A large cloud of dust erupted from the explosion. The steam-operated work whistle was tied down and continued to blast until it ran out of steam, for a final farewell to the end of an era.

Dance in the Old Girl Yet

Rats. Here we have a great project, the *Dreamer*, an Old 28' Twin-engine Chris Craft, all kinds of juicy possibilities, and old gloomy Common Sense steps in and spoils everything.

You might know; happens every time. Well, not every time, not if you're quick enough and act before you think of all the negatives, before old Common Sense sticks its head in the door and says, "You know a lot could go wrong with this. If I were you I'd quit."

"Shut-up!" There's your answer. Then take it from there.

You may remember the Dreamer, the old Queen Red Anderson and I bought last fall, sight unseen. Old, sure, and she needed everything but she reeked class. That old boat kept me busy all winter just thinking what we might do with her. Of course it would take money to bring her back to mint condition, we knew that and fresh paint, deck carpeting, darn the holes in her socks, some clean underwear maybe, but once brought back to her real beauty she could say with Mahitabel the Cat, "There's a Dance in the Old Girl Yet!"

Did I say it would take some money? Certainly, if we hired it done. Turns out a lot. And we'd do it right, do it all the way or not at all. I hadn't forgotten Julian Nelson's comment when I asked him 30 years ago, what he thought of my idea of buying the old 48' *Liberty* for $3,000. "I know the *Liberty*, Hale," He said. "The *Liberty* is an old wooden boat, and anybody who thinks an old wooden boat has improved with age has a wooden head!" Good advice and I took it, but where's the fun in good advice? Never mind, Julian and I are still friends.

Red and I already had a good boat of course, Bill Bloomer's 21' Starcraft the *Driftaway*, a sweet little Inboard-Outboard perfect for us and if we'd sold her and kept the *Dreamer* we wouldn't feel right about it I know. So I guess we'll sell the *Dreame*r as is. I can see Common Sense rubbing its hands.

I wrote those paragraphs yesterday, then lay awake half the night thinking of things a new owner of a classy old Chris Craft might do.

How about this? He could launch her and live on her. Why not? Beats buying and building a cabin on expensive and immovable lakeshore. Blades and I, with little Mexican dog, Spare Parts, and orphan tomcat, Fierce, sailed our 25' Swedish Diesel, the *Lida Rose*, from Houston, Tex. To Cornucopia, Wis. Lived on her all the way and loved it. That was in 1976; took us over four months, the best four months of my life.

Or he could run her as a Lake Superior chartered tour-and-trolling boat; she comes with enough tackle for every trout in the lake, and on days he's boating no fish, he can always cruise the Squaw Bay Caves, always there and always worth seeing.

Or he could take his time scrapping, painting and tuning up her twin 235-horsepower engines and then sell her back, at a hefty profit, to Red and me. We'd go for it sure. We know a good deal when we see one.

Doggone Mosquitoes and Little Boy Blue

I don't know what's happened with our Bark Bay mosquitoes. Too much soft living? I know the time when a fellow stepping out the door would get stabbed right there and be carried back to the swamp as a trophy, to make a good meal for three or four of them. As time went along they found it wiser to eat him right at the door; back in the swamp the big ones would get him.

Times have changed for sure. Not only no mosquitoes but in three weeks here I've picked off only two woodticks. Feel downright deprived and put upon. And neither Red nor I have caught a fish, probably because with all the rain we haven't been out.

Eight of the neat little birdhouses put up by Washburn's Ralph Wickdal along the Lost Creek stretch of Highway 13 about 25 years ago are still standing. He built them trying to bring back the bluebirds, having learned they must be a certain height with the entrance just big enough for a bluebird, not big enough for swallows.

Kind of sad, those houses standing empty. Driving by yesterday I thought of Eugene Field's poem about Little Boy Blue, who left his toys placed neatly on the shelf, went to bed and never woke up.

"The little toy soldier is covered with dust, but sturdy and staunch he stands. What has become of our Little Boy Blue?, they ask. Or Ralph Wickdal's bluebirds. Maybe some day they'll come back. Sure like to see that.

Doggone. While I'm complaining about no mosquitoes two land on me. Both made a smooth landing but it was their last. Thought for the day: Is there a sound more maddening than a mosquito about to land on your ear when you're just falling asleep?

Dense fog this morning; couldn't see the lake, only 75 feet from our door. Fifty-two degrees, and according to the TV weatherman, it will be 112 degrees in Phoenix. Which would you prefer? I'll take Bark Bay anytime.

Just talked with Judy Palm at her waterfront shop. "The Good Earth" who says "the slip is half-empty because the water's so low"

NOTES FROM THE HORN

lowest in over 70 years. The fellows can't launch their sailboats! It's rising though; we'll be O.K. soon. I know she's right. The town newsletter just in and this sleepy little village is really moving. Volunteers are doing cleanup. Dave Tillmans' new crane will be dredging the mouth of the Siskiwit River which silts up the marina, the harbor shops are all in business, and the old green shed is getting a fancy addition. From the newsletter: Green Shed: The Town approved the building of a 38'x39' shelter to be attached to the existing green shed at the lakefront. The roof will also have new roofing that extends over the food service area used at Cornucopia Day. The green shed was originally used as Ehlers' fish processing center when Cornucopia was in its prime.

The Town needs a shelter large enough for eight picnic tables and food service tables to be used for Cornucopia Day, family picnics and other summer gatherings. We are seeking donations to build the shelter, the Town will pay for remodeling needed to preserve the existing building.

Sleepy little village, my foot.

Compared to these murderous black biting flies Bark Bay mosquitoes are Victorian gentlemen.

A mosquito lands on you so gently you don't notice him, walks slowly around, testing here and there to make sure you qualify (I always do), then chooses his spot and sucks up his dinner. Provided of course, you haven't already swatted him.

But these flies! Brother. They could give a piranha lessons. On hot humid days they come by the millions, armed to the teeth and hot for the kill. This being a family newspaper I can't use the proper words to describe these devils but believe me, I do when I'm out of your hearing. Doesn't help of course; if I wear long thick woolen socks walking the beach they bite right through them. I think they bite through leather. A pox, a murrain of them!

Last night our raccoon, a regular visitor, walked up and came almost nose-to-nose with our cat, Kelly, who was snoozing on our walking plank. Both Coon and Kelly arched their backs and apparently exchanged a few words, then the coon slid away, no harm done. Sure wish I would have been quick enough to get a shot of that.

With our recent downpours we've had to wear boots getting to the car. Our Canada geese don't though; there were 23 of them clipping the lawn this morning. After the clipping they waddled down to the beach and squatted on the water's edge, where I took several pictures of them. Still have a few shots left on that roll; at this writing I have a camera full of sunsets, Horoznieckis and Canada geese, all native to the area.

Gave myself a South Shore tour the other day and we sure look good! In Port Wing every pole has a beautiful blue "Welcome to Port Wing" sign; they look great and the yards are so neat and colorful you want to stop at all of them. Same thing in Herbster; on the Lenawee Road just off the highway is the Community Hall, a big handsome building. Well-kept homes across the street, and a mile down the road the Isaksson Lumber Company, lumber stacked over several acres, evidence that this little town isn't entirely dependent on tourism.

Cornie is right in there too, and I think the comment in the recent newsletter about the time when Cornucopia was in its prime is a little off. It's in its prime, or very close to it, right now. Just had another successful Fish Fry and 4th of July fireworks by the way. (Mother Nature gave us some fireworks of her own later that night, absolutely free.)

The other day, Mark Ehlers, who runs Wisconsin's northernmost Certified Public Accountant's office, made me some copies of old maps by the French over 300 years ago. These maps show the whole lake including the Apostle Islands and Bark Bay. Gives me goose pimples thinking of those guys cruising along our beach, mapping it that long ago. When I was a kid some fellows digging for bait here, hit two hammered-copper kettles. I had one for years, don't know what happened to it but recently wrote the Wisconsin Historical Society in Madison about them. They said, "These were used by the French and English for trading with the Indians."

The history we live with and don't know!

Try the C-Side

The old show business line, "Give the people what they want and they'll turn out for it," holds in the restaurant business too. Try the C-Side on Thursday's spaghetti night, or the Friday night fish fry. Great food and lots of it. Wall-to-wall people.

I just found three unused Gillette razor blades in the old log cabind here, neatly wrapped in wax paper tucked in another neat wrapping and ready to go, if you could get to the blade without cutting your finger. I have no idea how old these are, I can say the blade I actually tried was a handsome bronze color but it was like shaving with a hacksaw.

I gave up on the second stroke and switched to the modern Gillette which comes in a tiny metal box; you slide the blade out with your thumb and geat a painless shave. But even these are about through — most fellows today use either an electric shaver or those little throwaways with a plastic handle. I'd better stock up before they and I are both obsolete.

The Hermit Wilson left a Fortune in Gold
Dec. 17, 1998

I've just received a huge package of 40-year old copies of the Bayfield Press from Dr. Leo Beebe, Fowler, Ind., last of the original Bayfield Pioneer family. I think I've seen Leo maybe three times since we were students at the University of Wisconsin in the early 1930s, no matter, he's not the type to forget old friends. He writes:

"Getting near Christmas, I many times have thought of our unusual trip in Clarence's Model T Ford, which we borrowed for the trip and where the low band burned out before even leaving Madion, but we pushed the car to get it going fast enough so we could use high gear. Remember, we left the car in Mellen and went the rest of the way by bus and picked up the car on our way back to Madison.

In this stack of old yellowed papers Leo so thoughtfully sent me there's enough Bayfield history, all of it written by old friend, Bill Knight's sister, Eleanor, who's no longer with us I'm sorry to say, to fill a book, a thick book, factual and good reading, at least for anyone who knows that country.

The ornery hermit Wilson (first name never mentioned) of Wilson Island, now on the chars as Hermit Island, who supposedly left a fortune in gold buried there, kept strangers off with his trusty rifle, his only real friend. When a courageous visiting Indian found him dead on the floor of his shack (of whisky it was thought) Bayfield people dug up the whole island looking for that gold which, for all I know is there yet.

English Can Be Beautiful

"There are no rules," my Mexican friend, Fedrico Hoyes, once told me, complaining about the English language. He had a point. If you know the punctuation rules of Spanish, you can read anything aloud and pronounce it correctly, allowing for your accent of course, and never mind that you can't translate what you've read. Can't do that in English though, there are rules but they are all full of exceptions. Suppose you said "I live for live TV." You wouldn't say "I lyve for liv TV" would you? Of course not. You might say "I baked, then raked the lawn naked," never "I bake-ed, then rake-ed the lawn nayt." Why not? Well for one thing, you would put some pants on.

Forgive me. *The County Journal* hasn't come in yet, so I don't know what's going on in the world.

Yesterday's *Wall Street Journal*, which Blades subscribes to and reads cover to cover (she makes money on stocks too), had an article headed "Power Point Goes to School." I read the whole thing and still don't know what Power Point is, some sort of computerized educational video game, I gather. This line caught my eye though, "When Public Agenda, a non-profit research group, recently asked employers what they thought of today's high school graduates, most said the younsters were handy with computers, but couldn't spell or write." Hah. I have the cure for that. Take them back to Miss White in the third grade, to Miss Olson in the fourth and on up to Miss Cowie in the eighth and they would write good English, spelled right, the rest of their lives. Keeping a dictionary handy at all times, of course.

Miss Cowie, (Freda Cowie but all teachers were Miss then, you would never use a first name), knew English. "Yes, Hale?" "That just sort of struck me funny." "Well, I suppose you couldn't help being struck funny." I have never used that expression since.

Something else, English can be beautiful. I think some memorable words stick with us because they have a musical rhythm. Lincoln's "We will nobly save, or meanly lose, this last, best hope of earth." Or Stonewall Jackson's dying words, "Let us cross over the river, and rest in the shade of the trees." Washington, "We have fought through the war together. My heart is too full to say more."

Thanks. I have more, but the mail's coming in.

Gone With The Wind

Clark Gable. Know that name, do you? O.K., you're old enough for this.

In 1944 I was a cook in the Merchant Marines, A few more cooks like me and the Japanese might have won the war, but never mind that. I had just signed off the tanker Cat's Paw, in San Pedro after four months in the Pacific and, wearing my Sheepshead Bay Navy type uniform which I thought might help, was hitch-hiking to the cabin in the Santa Susanna mountains where my wife and little daughter were waiting out the war.

A red 1940 Packard coupe stopped for me, I opened the door and there, wearing a big grin, was what was probably the most recognizable face in the world, certainly in the "Gone With the Wind" United States.

"Aren't you Clark Gable?"

"Yes," he said, seeming to get a kick out of it himself.

I scrambled in before he could change his mind and said something I can't believe yet. "My name's O'Malley, I suppose you've heard of me." I hate to admit it but that's what I said, and I'm sure the man said to himself, "My-God what-have-I-got-here?" But we started talking about the war. He had just done a hitch with the Air Force and I relaxed a little. I even forgot, sort of, that I was riding with Clark Gable and I could see he was perfectly at ease talking with the famous Hale O'Malley, Chief Cook on the tanker *Cat's Paw*.

We had something in common here. He was making a movie in which he was one of the crew on a merchant ship. "I play a bo's'un," he said, and said bo's'un not boatswain. I had, an hour before, left ours on the Callabee, drunk as a skunk, but, down to earth now, kept my big mouth shut.I saw that show later and remember the ad, "Gable's Back and Garson's Got Him!" Show wasn't his best by far.Ah, yes. Forty-nine years ago, and I bet I haven't worked that 30-minute ride into conversations more than three thousand times since.

I did, I'm happy to remember, have the grace not to ask for his autograph, but just before he dropped me off at Chatsworth I said, "It must be kind of a nuisance for you, Mr. Gable, not to even be able to go in a drugstore for a pack of cigarettes without people swarming all over you."

"Yes," he said. "But the compensation is good!" Same grin.

We parted, I like to think, friends, and on my next ship, the *Cat's Paw*, I raised one of those thin black Clark Gable mustaches. I looked terrific, but as I tell my friends to this day, once back in the States I had to shave it off. It was hurting his career. People kept running up to him, all excited, "Aren't you Hale O'Malley?"

Might as well tell them that, it's harmless, and I know they don't believe I ever rode with Clark Gable anyway.

I did though.

Ground Hog Day has Come and Gone

What, oh what are we coming to? Groundhog Day is here and gone and not a word in the Phoenix paper about it. Not a word! The next issue of *The County Journal* will be here today and if there's no mention of this famous milestone, especially in Cornucopia where, years ago, Poncho Roman of Poncho's famous tavern said, one February second, "Jack, your wife's on the phone. "Tell her we're celebrating Groundhogs' Day." Which for years afterward and I hope still do, they have. If not I guess we'll just have to fold our tents and admit The End Is Near.

Two month's ago I left my new bike unattended for 45 seconds while I stepped around the corner to mail a letter and in that short time it was stolen. And now even in Northern Wisconsin: a couple from up there stopped in yesterday and when they left the lady said, "Don't put our names in the paper! They'll know the house is vacant."

So I haven't.

Here in Arizona we have all kinds of hummingbirds, some of which stay with us all year keeping Blades busy filling the glass feeders. Yesterday a little fellow got caught behind the sliding screen door, injured his wing and fell to the ground. I locked Kelly the cat in the house, picked him up and put him on a towel on the patio table, but he didn't make it. I've read a hummingbird's metabolism and heartbeat are a hundred times ours and they have to refuel constantly, so this little guy didn't have a chance.

When he died I got out the book and looked him up; he was an Anna's Hummingbird beautiful green back and a really striking iridescent red head.

A couple of my friends are atheists, or think they are. All life is just an accidental combination of chemicals, they say. "Have your chemicals build me a hummingbird," I say, loving the argument since I feel I have all the ammunition.

To twist the knife a little I sometimes add, "Every coin and bill in your pocket from a penny up says 'In God We Trust' and you don't want to be carrying around stuff like that. Give it to me." But they never do. This kind of argument is fun though since neither of us can prove anything.

Never mind. I still think the hummingbirds and I are holding all the cards.

Hanky Panky Banking
Bayfield County Press, Professor Pulpwood

One of the unique advantages of living in Cornucopia is that we don't need calendars. When we see Morty in town it's Monday. Albert Lawin heading for the wholesaler's in Duluth it's Tuesday. Wednesday is open. Thursday, Shorty Englund and Lloyd Bloom from Bayfield and Doc Gibbons from Ashland. Friday Hugh and Donna Swanson from Minneapolis, Saturday every trailer and camper in Wisconsin, Sunday Roger on the Lowrey organ. A while ago Shorty and Lloyd missed their day and we had two Wednesdays that week but other than that we have as good a system as you'd want.

Travelers making it as far as Port Wing will be happy to know that the former co-op store on 13 there is in business again as an IGA affiliate under the management of Ralph Swanson, former resident of Port Wing. Anyone ranging farther west than that comes to Jardine's which Press subscribers are advised is about as far as they should go in these troubled times. Good place to stop and water the horses though.

Lament for the dear, dead days heard in Bayfield the other day: "These fancy clocks and computers in banks may be O.K. but there was no hanky-panky banking when Joe O'Malley ran the place." We agree. Few things worse than hanky-panky-banking.

More than No Hunting and No Trespassing signs around here than we've ever seen before. Goes with the increased tourist traffic we suppose but we're thinking of putting up a few "Trespassers Welcome" and "Hunt your Fool Head Off" signs just to counteract the impression. We aren't really that ornery. Oh well I don't know. Maybe we are.

A lakeshore cottage owner had this note written on a map of Bayfield County stuck in his door the other day: "You own this whole shoreline and you won't let a needy married couple spend a couple of days here, my wife is in tears and we have no place to go. Thanks a hell of a lot!" Well, I really can't blame that poor wife. If I was stuck with a horse's patootie like that I'd be in tears myself.

If you happened to be outside and looking up on a Saturday night about three weeks ago, along about three weeks ago, along about 2 or 3 a.m., you saw one of our fanciest displays of Northern Lights. Covered half the sky. Of course if you're one of those who've forgotten what Saturday nights are for we can do nothing for you except pass along this warning to stay up after this. No telling what you might be missing.

Headline we'd enjoy: "Dear Abby Runs Off With Married Man."

We visit the Marina in Bayfield regularly and see it's changing for the better every day. A few years ago one sailboat in the bay was a rarity, now you see a dozen at a time anytime. And Marina manager Jim Miller says he's lost 12 pounds just running back and forth taking care of the customers. We knew Jim when he was so thin that when he turned sideways you didn't see him at all. We hope his business doesn't get that good, or that bad, again.

Word just in that the family pig has died and we must go to Ireland to settle the estate. See you sometime.

Morty Sez: Courtesy is costless.

And from Roger O'Malley: Congratulations to the lucky people who managed to acquire Bobbie's kittens, Shirley, Goodness, Mercy and Will. May they follow their new owners all the days of their nine lives.

He'll Never get to Tennessee

I see the Department of Natural Resources along with some other government agencies has trapped live fishers and sent twenty of them to Tennessee. I never heard of this vicious animal, which apparently kills anything smaller than itself, till a few years ago, and have seen only two (they are like a large black weasel), but Eric Sharp's article says the state introduced them to our Chequamegon National Forest in the 1960s. Is that why we don't see porcupines anymore, and rarely a rabbit, a woodchuck, a fox or raccoon? They're death on cats too, and we have a cat.

I don't take pleasure in killing anything, but I'm a pretty good shot with my Browning .22 and if I see one of those devils at Bark Bay next summer, he'll never get to Tennessee.

I haven't heard, but Randy Krause's handsome new store and service station in Corny should be having its grand opening about now. This is a great thing for Cornucopia and we sure wish him all the luck in the world. The building itself looks so good, and not having to drive miles out of town to get gas will be really something.

It takes courage to take on a project like this, always a gamble and a long wait to get your investment back. I don't know what besides gas and oil Randy will sell, but I haven't forgotten his grading our Bark Bay driveway. If he hadn't, we couldn't get in or out, after he had already put in a hard day, and whatever he sells we will buy.

From the Washburn Police Report: "Complaint that a resident at an apartment complex has a pit-bull type dog, which is prohibited in the city limits. Officer arrived and found that the dog is not a pit-bull."

"Report of a female putting garbage from her car into a city dumpster."

"Report of a missing purse. Complainant later called to report she had found her purse."

I miss the reports that had a little mystery, that left you wondering how they came out. What happened to the fellow found locked in the post office a year or two ago? How about the lady who called to report a dead bear in the road and was advised "Put him in a pickup and take him to a freezer." Did she have a pickup truck? Did she lift that bear into it all by herself? Where did she find a freezer big enough for a dead bear?

"I have had many troubles in my life, most of which never happened."_ Mark Twain.

Here in Cornie They are All Over the Place

"There you are," said the cheerful young driver as he climbed back in his big ten-wheel truck. "Have a nice day!," and off he went, having just laid a load of two-inch rock on the steep end of our Bark Bay driveway and needing four runs to get back over it and up the hill. Once up, he told me with a smile. "You'll never make it with your car." And he was almost right, but you can't talk to Terry and Shirley Welt's '91 Cadillac that way. Getting up a good head of steam, we lurched and bounced over those stone heaps and made it, just made it, leaving Marion's old Dodge van dry-docked, bottom of the hill.

I'd had a nice day but his wasn't it. I'd called Olson Brothers in Brule for a load of stone big enough to not wash away in our heavy rains. In my innocence, thinking I would be instantly able to drive on it. I could all right, in a Sherman tank. He had laid it as evenly as he could up the hill, which was all he was supposed to do. But it lay very thick in some spots. "You'll have to get somebody with a grader or cat," he told me.

Now what? Ah. A fellow named Randy Krause is building a store and service station just up from Ehlers' in Cornie and I'd seen a lot of heavy machinery there, one piece a tank-tread Bob Cat. I drove in and luckily Randy was there. At four o'clock, he'd already had a long day. "Yeah, I'll come out, gotta finish up here though, be two-three hours." Since it would be pretty late, nearly dark, I didn't really expect him at all, but at seven there he was, pushing stone with his little cat, not only smoothing the hill, but as I saw next morning, clear back to the highway.

I paid Randy what he asked and a little more, the total being about a third of what it should have been.

What about people like this? We'll be back in Phoenix in a few days, population there some two million, with no doubt plenty of Randy Krauses. Trouble is you have to find them. Here in Cornie they are all over the place.

Hale O'Malley

How May I Help You ?

Technology, we are really moving. Call any business these days, you don't get a person, you get a polite recorded voice. "Thank you for calling Hi-Fly Airlines. Please select one of the following nine options. If you are calling about incoming flights, press one. If you are calling about departing flights, press two. If you are calling about our special eight-day tourist-class no-return offer press"... and so on. If you can tough it out, you eventually, eventually, get a real live person, bright and cheerful as a morning in May. "Hi, this is Marilyn. How may I help you?" But you have forgotten what you called about.

We are all inclined to remember the good old days as better than today, but darned if in some ways they weren't. When my mother died, years ago, dad lived alone in the beautiful Bayfield home he had built for $3,500 in 1910 and in which I was born in 1914. I kept in regular touch with him by phone from St. Paul.

"Number please." (Helen Cease, operator for years, she had known me since I was born.) "Seven-one-J." "No, your dad isn't home, Hale. I saw him walk by the bank awhile ago. He'll be meeting Doug and Shine at the tavern. I'll try George's."

You don't get that kind of service anymore. Not possible, too many people. Once, listening to a recorded, I thought, litany of press-one, press-two... I made an exasperated improper, well all right, obscene suggestion. "Excuse me?" A live female person. I have never completely recovered. I hope she has. Luckily this was before caller I.D. You can't be too careful these days.

At the suggestion of a few of you, I hope to compile some of these Notes into a little North Country book, and Red Anderson has just talked with *The County Journal* people about it. They have agreed to let Red cull the last five years' issues for any worth reprinting. A tedious job for which I have agreed to pay. With that, and some columns saved by Barbara Jonas, Nancy Raeburn, and Lynn Louden, a good friend from Oakland, California we knew in Mexico, I hope to come up with something, I hope fairly soon.

I keep going back to that house where I was born and grew up, built in 1910 for $3,500 as I say, and finally paid for 30 years later. I wonder if Paul Erickson's name, "Paul R. Erickson," the R for his middle name, Arthur, is still on the board supporting the back porch where he carved it 80 years ago. I hope it is.

The concrete block foundation supporting the room we called the alcove formed a little dirt-floor space we could crawl into, where one missing block left an opening big enough for single-digit-aged kids. Of course, we organized a club there and I still remember John Sherwood's initiation. John was about seven and if that dank, dirt-floored dark and tiny room wasn't enough to scare anybody, my brother Roger's get up as Initiating Officer sure was. He had a black hood over his head and a long black stocking covering his right arm, stuck out to welcome John, who started to cry, as anybody would.

Knowing we were asking for trouble with our folks, especially John's folks, the club disbanded. Next summer though, I'm going to ask if I can peek under the porch to see if that one-block opening is still there. Just peek, I wouldn't think of trying to squeeze in. Place is full of ghosts.

I Know When I'm Licked Sept. 19, 2002

Early September, still warm, and the flies have taken over. Last night I must have swatted fifty. They like to bed down on the ceiling, one of the things they can do that we can't, and for the moment, they are easy marks. No matter, come morning the place is buzzing with three times as many, who knows where they come from? And Marion and I are batting away, half the time swatting the spot they just left.

How come flies are so fast? We humans think we have the best brains in the kingdom, so when we decide to swat a fly, the brain instructs the nerves and muscles to wind up and swat, all this very, very fast. So we swat and hit where they were, they being smarter at the game.

I was awakened at dawn by one fly, seemed like ten but only one, practicing takeoffs and landings on my nose and forehead and giving me a choice between pulling the covers over my head and suffocating, or foolishly trying to slap him, risking a bloody nose or a fractured skull. No use. Six more touch-and-go landings and I got up. I know when I'm licked.

NOTES FROM THE HORN

I'll Never Make the Big Leagues

I have been watching baseball on TV and finally realize it's true, I will never make the big leagues. Probably not even the minors. The problems: I have never chewed bubble gum, wouldn't even know how to blow a bubble if I did. I don't scratch much, spit very seldom and never in public, let alone on TV. This last failing alone would keep me out for sure. I just watched a Milwaukee Brewers player with a long lead off first spit four times in three seconds and he wasn't chewing anything. Plus all that, in my best days at Bayfield, now at 88 long gone, I couldn't field worth a hoot and next to Louie Laesig, was the worst hitter they had. Ah, well. I still have this job with *The County Journal*.

The bill from Chequamegon Telephone Company always includes a list of new subscribers and this last one shows a new phone at Corny, North Point Station. Can't wait to see who or what that is. Called, but no answer. We will be there late June and I'll report.

Scott just called and said Larry Luoma just died. Good man. I have known him for years. Sure sorry to lose him.

So Bayfield has a Lions Club. A good outfit. Their motto is "We Serve," and this one will too. I have belonged to the Lions in St. Paul, Port Wing and Puerto Renasco, Mexico, where I was sort of their token gringo. The membership was the elite of the town. I was happy to be accepted and made some good friends. Played poker my first night and won three dollars and fifty cents, and the next day the Mexican crew building my first house not only knew I had played and won, but knew exactly how much. Got a big kick out of it.

Those Mexicans were lively. The rapid Spanish was too much for me but I participated as best I could. I still remember our Chinese-Mexican banker, Jesus "Chuy" Leji, coming to our beach trailer. "'ow many teekits you want for the barbecue?" "Two I suppose. I didn't know we were having a barbeque." "You voted for it."

They met every week and had regular picnics and parties. It got to be a little much. A great experience though. I think a Lions Club will be a real asset to Bayfield.

The Washburn police report is usually a good source of items for this column, but not lately. Dog tearing garbage bags, car or two in the ditch, a few liquored-up tavern scufflings. I think I'll rest until we are at Bark Bay in June. I can depend on our mergansers, Canada geese and bald eagles plus the deer and an occasional bear for news, and they all like to see their names in the paper. See you then.

I Think I'll Play it Over Tonight

"Some day I'm going to murder the bugler. Some day they're going to find him dead, and then I'll get that other pup, the guy who wakes the bugler up, and spend the rest of my life in bed."

I'm sure when Irving Berlin wrote that sprightly WWI tune in 1917, and sang it in the Broadway play, "Yap, Yap Yaphank" he didn't have me in mind. I wasn't yet three and we had never met, but if he were writing it today, it would sure fit. This daily fast and painless dose of radiation really tires you out. I shuffle around a little every morning hoping this passes for exercise, but in a few minutes, brother, does that bed look good. And back I go.

On the wall facing my bed we have a large photo of a tiger, his life-sized yellow-eyed head staring straight at me day and night. I've always respected him, anybody would, and have come to admire him. More than that, as we study each other, I've come to see him as a friend and it wouldn't surprise me a bit, one of these half-asleep nights, to have him step out of the frame and pad over to sit by my bed, where I could scratch his ears.

I've carried this pleasant scenario a little further. We shuffle off the earth at the same time and are standing at the pearly gates to be interviewed by Saint Peter.

"You're Hale O'Malley? Hm. Who's your friend, Mr. O'Malley?" Tiger raises his head and gives Saint Peter his yellow-eyed, thousand-yard stare which says, plain as day, "Who wants to know, bub?" Pete's no fool. "Go right in, fellows," he says. "They'll measure you for your wings."

Knowing no self-respecting jungle cat would put up with the indignity of fake angel wings, I close off my fantasy at this point. Sure enjoy it though. We both do.

I think I'll play it over tonight.

Just as well we stayed in Arizona.

"Darned if I don't think that's unconstitutional."
"Right. You've read the constitution?"
"Well, not lately. Well, no."
We have a lot in common. A little book at my elbow as I write, put out by the CATO Institution, not much bigger than a deck of cards and a lot thinner, has the Declaration of Independence and the full text of the Constitution and I'm going to read both this very day. Later today, but today for sure. Well, pretty sure.

Next day. Sorry, I suppose most of us are determined to read, when we have time of course, what we have always felt we should but haven't. I actually read the whole Bible once, but you can't speed read the Bible and right now I'm trying again but only one chapter at a time. This will take months. I've made it through Genesis and am ploughing my way through Exodus but it isn't easy. The Lord gave Moses such detailed, precise instructions on building the Ark of the Covenant, and everything to be covered with pure gold. How did they mine all that gold, in 1500 B.C.? The book doesn't say but I'll keep reading and if there's any mention of it, I'll let you know. I'm too quick to question. Better stick with glacial kettles.

Jeff Greene of the Herbster post office has just forwarded our back mail, including three issues of *The County Journal* and I am always amazed at all the social and community action up there. The Bayfield Apple Festival alone tired me out and we weren't even there. Wouldn't have found a place to park anyway. Just the same, I would still like to have played trumpet in their parade, especially since I believe the parade route was all downhill, very important when you are eighty-seven.

Just as well we stayed in Arizona.

Woodcocks, Mosquitos and Ticks

A recent Dick Ellis story on the game bird woodcock in this paper was really informative. I didn't know there was a fall woodcock migration, let alone a season on them, in Wisconsin this year Sept. 21 through Nov. 4. They weigh, I learn, an average of 7.6 for females, 6.2 for males so you must have to pick and clean quite a few to get a decent meal. We've given them a lot of names too: Timberdoodle, Night Partridge, Big Eye, Bog Sucker, Mud Snipe. Good grief. I've seen only one in my life and that's when I was a kid walking through the woods about 75 years ago and a rocket exploded under my feet and shot out of sight. I'd read the Burgess Bird Book so I knew what it was. A woodcock.

This article answered for me something I had wondered about for years. I'd read that they probe for earthworms with a beak nearly three inches long, and "they can probe the ground and open the end of the bill without opening the entire bill," according to DNR ecologist Keith Warnke. "It works on a type of hinge."

My gosh. I was never sure if I'd read that or imagined it but here it is in *The County Journal* and that's all you need. Mother Nature sure does come up with some neat tricks. For example, did you ever study a porcupine quill? No needle was ever so sharp, and when he whacks it into you with that bristling tail, it stays there, the tip is serrated. Ask any educated dog.

Ticks now. Woodticks. They are born knowing the way to get dinner is to hang on a blade or stalk with one set of legs and the other three stretched in the air so when you walk by, they can swing aboard for a free ride and with luck a meal.

You usually feel a tick and pick him off before he sinks his jaws into you and settles down for a long drink of your blood, but once he's in, he's in for keeps and when you finally find him and pull him out a piece of your hide comes too, and that bite will itch something fierce. Mosquitoes aren't in it with ticks. I know.

How did I get on this? I thought I was writing about woodcocks.

Nuts oh Geez!

If I hear once more, just one more, self-anointed intellectual pontificating on TV say "and at this point in time," I'm going to throw a shoe right through the tube. That portentous phrase originated with Mr. John Dean at the Nixon Watergate investigation, which went on almost as long as the Joe McCarthy thing, another guy I could do without. In fact it pleases me to recall that I'd pegged Senator McCarthy as a real phony early on, one of the few times in such matters I wasn't wrong. "At this point in time." Nuts.

Well, this is no way to start a column intended to be what we might call light reading. Cheerful. Easy. No strain. No deep thinking. All right, now as soon as I can interview the owners, and I don't even have their names yet, of the fantastic lodge going up on Siskiwit Bay just north of Cornie, I'll do a whole column on it.

Roy and Elaine Jacobson took us out there the other day; neither we nor Cornucopia have seen anything like it. Really. Top shelf all the way. About a dozen guest rooms all with lake view, all with fireplaces, one with a Jacuzzi. Full complimentary breakfast every morning. Brother! It isn't completed yet, but when it is I think I'll ask Marion to marry me again so, assuming she accepts, I can take her there for a second honeymoon. Of course, then getting her back to our little trailer on the beach might be a problem, but I'll face that when I come to it. Why borrow trouble?

That place is going to put Cornie on the map like nothing ever has. I know it.

You see some pretty fancy craft in our Marina these days but none more impressive than Dr. Joe Horozaniecke's spanking new Boston whaler he's named the "Roger O" after my brother Roger who left us Nov. 8, 1990, but thanks partly to good friend Joe, is in a real sense still with us.

Joe and Mary had a christening service at the harbor, a dedication by Roger's widow Barbara, followed by a party at their house on Squaw Point. Red Anderson and I contributed the 8-pound laker we'd caught off Roman Point the day before, and the next day son,

Scott and I followed Joe, Mary and daughter, Sherrie, out of the harbor and took some pictures. Our *Drift Away* is a pretty fast boat, but when Joe kicked in that 225-horse outboard he shot out of sight and we haven't seen him since. I trust all is well with him.

Just now two fellows rowed in here wanting to know where all those big northerns I wrote about were hiding. I see the boys are still out there, casting. I wish them luck. For my money they're welcome to every northern pike in Lake Superior. At this point in time. Oh, geez.

One More Good Trout Day Maybe Two

I've paid my dues and except for periodic checkups against cancer recurrence, I am back to living. I sure owe a big debt of thanks to all those who wrote wishing me well. It really helped.

Now to matters of importance. Knowing how vital tourism is to the health of my home country, I have been promoting the value of our glacial kettles just off County C between Cornie and Washburn for years. Stirred some mild interest here and there and the county put out a little folder on them, but that was it until just a year ago. David Bratley of Washburn wrote me. Here's part of his letter: "March 28, 2002: On Nov. 6, Leon Solberg and I visited the glacial kettles off the Jodi Road parking lot. We both walked down to the bottom of the kettle. We took the four-wheeler trail down where we saw many old tires and broken bathroom appliances (toilets, etc.) had been thrown and rolled down the hill.

Suppose it was fun to see them roll down a steep incline. I talked to the Bay Area Active Sports Alliance (BAASA) thinking this might be a good cleanup project for them, but they referred me to the Bayfield County Forest Supervisor Paul Lundberg. I contacted his office about it and later, John Mesko called me, was very interested, and assured me they would gladly clean it up this spring. That's where it presently stands. Sort of disgusting people would do this and thought you would like to know."

This worked. The junk has been cleaned up. Must have been an awful job. And a few days ago, Dave sent me an application for a Wildlife Trail being planned in Madison, this trail to take in the whole state including the northern tier of 18 counties. Looks like a natural for us so I wrote them at once and am waiting to hear. He says they hope to be in business by October.

I've been out of touch with the South Shore too long. I don't even know if Randy Krause has opened his neat new service station and store just built in downtown Cornucopia. I sure wish him success. I haven't forgotten that after a long day's work there last summer, he drove out in his little Cat and spent the evening leveling the gravel in our Bark Bay driveway, dropped there in such a heap you couldn't get over it. Charged me about half the job was worth.

Sure hope to get back there this summer. Lake Superior owes me and Red and the *Driftaway* at least one more good trout day, maybe two. The fish we haven't caught the last six years must be pretty big by now.

Hale O'Malley

Outwit a Duck

I've been wondering how our editor and sports writer Darrell Pendergrass can report in detail every athletic contest in Bayfield County as he does, even when different games are played in different towns apparently on the same night. Then you turn the page and find he's been duck hunting all the time in some bog near Grand View.

I won't press him on this; I like my job. "The hunter crouches in his blind 'neath camouflage of every kind

And conjures up in a
quacking noise
To lend allure to his decoys
This grownup man,
with pluck and luck
Is hoping to outwit a duck

Well he does, and us, too.

In today's mail, from Harvey Hadland (that's a Bayfield name) via Greg and Gail Kinney a yellowed and fragile copy of the Bayfield Press dated January 4, 1934. Nineteen thirty-four! And on the front page is a long column by someone calling himself "The Lookout" and darned if that wasn't me! Good Grief. In it I was interviewing the fellows from our class of '32 and asking their plans for the future, "Balance the budget" Wally Nordin said, and we might have done that too, if we hadn't had to drop everything to fight World War II and then hurry back to raise a family and make a living. Sixty-four years ago. Ah well.

This old paper is great. The government had just guaranteed all depositors including those of Bayfield's First National Bank that their money was insured "up to $2,500" which at that time in Bayfield was flattery. Nobody in town had anywhere near that kind of money except maybe Henry Wachsmuth. He owned the bank.

My dad, Joe O'Malley, was bank president and was always

NOTES FROM THE HORN

proud that the First National, unlike hundreds of others in the country, never went under. I think I'll send *The County Journal* this paper. The bank had a full-page ad announcing this glorious news, but you know things haven't changed all that much. I think deposits now are insured up to $100,000, but a good car today costs about $30,000. In 1934 you bought one for a little over $400. That's if you had $400.

Bob Hadland called to tell me the lovely girl shown lighting my dad's cigar here awhile ago is Gerry LaPointe, Harry LaPointe's daughter. "I went to school with her," he said. "The boat in the background of that shot is Joe LeBel's *Fair Lady*. You can also see part of Jack Moon's *Moon's Troller #1*.

Thanks, Bob. Glad to have that cleared up.

Of course I remember Harry LaPointe. Harry moved to Los Angeles and had a restaurant there; I had lunch there in 1944 or '45, can't recall what I ordered but I know it was good.

Joe LeBel I knew very well. Knew the whole family, but checking the phone book just now I don't find any LeBels still in Bayfield, darn it. Joe was always working something; built a handsome iceboat one year and I remember his taking our Mayor Anton Lindquist for a ride. Whipping along over glare ice the wind put him in a sharp turn and Anton slid off. He skidded about 40 feet on his back, no harm done but that was the last of his iceboating.

Bayfield's "Strawberry Regatta" in those days featured a trolling boat race: the Fair Lady always won so they finally cancelled the event. It was either that or scuttle the Fair Lady.

Joe also invented, 50 years ago, a fish filleting machine, the precursor, I suppose, of the $50,000 machine Dean Halverson now has at Cornie.

Phone call from Red Anderson, partner in the old 28-foot Chris Craft we bought sight unseen. She's at Craig Johnson's Herbster Marina, looking good he says. Craig is going to check her over; we're keeping our fingers crossed.

Be glad you're living where you are. I drive a three-year-old Cadillac Sedan de Ville, bought used of course, and since she's just racked up 58,000 miles I thought I'd better bring her into the dealer for a checkup. "Should cost about a hundred," I thought, "so they'll charge me two. Okay." Wrong. Four hundred sixty-dollars and ninety-six cents. But since they had to keep her all day they drove me home in a limousine, and in late afternoon came out to bring me back to the shop in their fancy new van, just on the market and which with optional TV — honest — sells for $55,000. (A salesman told me they sold 10 of them the first day they came out. Of course, salesmen do exaggerate; I know, I've been one all my life, but I think this fellow told the plain truth).

Good Grief. The only new car I ever bought was a Cadillac Sedan De Ville from Egan in Ashland in 1977 and we're driving it yet. cost $11,000. Walking around the dealership here yesterday, I saw the same model, $43,000. My $460 tune up looks like a bargain.

Now I didn't write, as *The County Journal* had it 'As a born doityourselfer' I wrote 'As a born doityoursomebodyelser.'

Wanted to get it right.

When I wrote a check to the Cadillac cashier she said, "May I see your driver's license?" So I grumbled back to my car and got my driver's license. Shortly before that I wanted to cash a small check at the bank I deal with all the time. Showed the girl My Bank Card which is supposed to clear you from everything "Do you have a photo ID?," she said.

Be glad you're living where you are.

Quite an Adventure

My good wife (Marion Corning of Washburn, before I came along) says, "You're living in the past!" She's right of course, since that's the only place I've ever been. I'd like to live in the future but the future's no sooner here than it whips through the present and becomes the past. Doesn't seem fair, but you've probably observed this yourself. In any case there you are.

Part of the past I like to remember is the opening of the Bayfield Marina, in 1970 I think, when Jim and Marge Miller were the only ones with the foresight and courage to tackle suck a risky project. (The very word marina wasn't even in the dictionary then. It is now though, I've just looked it up. "Marina: harbor for pleasure craft,")

I know Marge kept a scrapbook on the marina story and I've asked her to write it for us —I'd do it myself but she's the authority. What I particularly remember now is talking to Jim about buying a boat.

"I just got a brochure on the very boat you should have," he said. "*The Albin*. Little two-cylinder 25-foot diesel. Made in Sweden, sold in Cos Cob, Connecticut. Costs about $10,000. I'll throw in a lot of extra equipment."

I'd never heard of the *Albin* or for that matter Cos Cob, Connecticut.

"I'll take it," I said, "but we aren't having it shipped out here. You're going back there with me and we're going to sail it here or no deal."

"I can't do that. We just opened this marina."

"Then we have no deal."

"I can do it." So we did. (Marge didn't divorce him on the spot but I think it was in the air).

The run from Long Island Sound to Lake Superior was a real adventure and I suppose it's just as well I can't recall all the details; I might have given up boating for keeps. Never mind; we made it. Through the Harlem River across the top of Manhattan to the Hudson, up the Hudson to a left turn at Troy and into the Erie

Canal, now called the New York Barge Canal; up and through 20-some locks to Oswego and Lake Ontario, across to Canada and into the Trent-Severn Canal which I'd never heard of but it's there on the charts. Into Port Severn on Lake Huron's Georgian Bay, then an all-night run to Detour Village and up to the Soo Lock. (I'd almost run us on the rocks off Drummond Island but never mind that). We made it, nobody got divorced, we kept the Cat's Paw (named after the merchant ship on which I'd single-handedly won World War II) in the Bayfield Marina for three years, sold it, bought another in Houston, Texas, and Marion and I ran that one, the Lida Rose, back to Bayfield too.

Cos Cob to Bayfield two weeks, Houston to Bayfield four-and-a-half months and if all this is living in the past, well, by golly it was living.

I wish I'd kept a log of that first trip with Jim; I did on the Houston trip and wrote it up for a boating magazine, "4,500 Miles Under Power." Still have a few copies if you'd like one. I'd make that trip again in a New York Minute but Marion says I'm too old. Women! Anyway right now I'm busy creating the Glacial Kettle Park off County Road C and can't spare the time. Sorry. More on marinas later if I hear from Marge Miller.

Radio's Still With Us

I have just read that this past summer was the hottest Phoenix ever had, 115 days over 100 degrees, 28 of them 110 degrees or more. I should smile. On every one of those days, we were on the beach at Bark Bay in the nicest summer yet, days warm and sunny, just enough rain and that mostly at night. Had some great lightning displays and even the northern lights a few times. Scott is clearing space for a cabin on the bluff so we had plenty of wood for evening beach fires. Doggone, thinking about it I sometimes wonder why we come south at all. I suppose if I take a trip back for a week in 20 below January, I'll remember.

Have you been getting those big sheets of stick-on labels with your name and address? Of course you have, all in thick envelopes announcing "Your Free Gift Enclosed". Free gift. And always an urgent request for money for some good cause or other. You feel a little cheap keeping the labels and sending nothing, so sometimes you write a check to clear your conscience. They bank on that and keep you on the list.

As a child of the depression, the real depression of the thirties, not the little flutterings we have had occasionally since, I can't make myself throw anything away. So I have kept all these handy free gift labels and yesterday peeled and stuck them, one by one, on the return address corner of at least 400 envelopes. Waste not, want not. Stamps cost 37 cents though.

The older I get, the surer I am that this amazing computerized, e-mailed, faxed, websited and dot-commed world we have created does more to us than for us. I have just spent two hours trying to hook up a phone amplifier to help my hearing. I hear but don't understand. I have to yell for Marion to take the phone. I finally sent for a Qwest service man who couldn't make it work either. Said it was defective. Maybe it is, more likely I am.

These wonderful inventions complicate your life. When I was a little kid, folks used to gather around the piano, Mom played fine piano, and sang. It was great. Then radio came along and it was

"Clara, Lou and Em," "One Man's Family," "Little Orphan Annie," "The Lone Ranger," "Jack Armstrong, the All American Boy," and of course "Amos 'n Andy". Everybody but everybody tuned in and went around imitating, Amos "n" Andy. No more singing around the piano. Radio's still with us, you have one in your car, don't you? Of course you do, and now TV. Is there a home in the USA with no TV? Perish the thought. Visit a friend, you exchange how-are-you's then sit, no talking, and watch TV. Never mind what you watch, anything will do. I'd go on with this, but there's a ball game on I have to see and besides my cell phone's ringing. I'll get Marion.

We no sooner got back to Arizona than word came that Joan Cook, good Washburn friend, had a heart attack and died. Really a shock. Joan was full of fun, always game to go, always good company. You expect somehow to get used to these gaps in the ranks, but we don't and I don't think we should. We will sure miss Joan.

Kansas City Nighthawks

The World Passing By.
No question about it. None.
The world isn't just passing me by, I've seen that for quite a while now, it has passed me by.

I'm way back, hopefully treading water while I bob pitifully in its wake. For example, I probably own the last manual typewriter still in service (I'm typing this on it right now, mistakes and all) and the last time it needed a ribbon I bought two, just to play it safe.

When I went to the huge Office Max store here yesterday for a supply of the copy paper called "onion skin" I was politely told: "Sorry, we no longer stock it." And was sold 500 sheets of plain typing paper I didn't need. I could use more carbon paper. But was afraid to ask for it.

Good grief. When I was a kid the radio was just coming in (before that people gathered around the piano and sang) and I remember those boxy Atwater-Kent sets with a dozen important-looking dials nobody understood. Frank "FM" Herrick, brought one to the house and I remember everyone crowding around while he twisted the dials and got nothing. "Gee, if we could only get some noise!" Roger said, he was eight.

Later, when we had our cigar-box-size little Radiola with two head sets Roger had a big diagram listing all the stations he'd picked up. KDKA Pittsburgh came in best as I recall. He got Kansas City, too.

With the Coon-Sanders band — the Kansas City Nighthawks. (Years later, during the Depression, that band played at the Bayfield Pavilion).

I well remember Currie Bell and I listening to Grahm McNamee announcing the famous long-count Dempsey-Tunney fight in Chicago on that little set; "Tunney is down! Tunney is down!" I can hear him yet. That was 1927.

FAX? E-mail? Web Site? We wrote letters, long hand, and you didn't make a long distance phone call unless it was about something important, like a new baby or a death in the family.

Then, to make a call, you turned a little crank and got a human being, the operator "central" who in Bayfield was Helen Cease. There was a song about a little girl trying to reach her daddy who had died, "Hello Central, Give Me Heaven." Never mind. Wasn't much of a song.

Is everything moving so much faster, or am I just slowing down? Both — I think. I bought Marion an electric typewriter a few years ago, already obsolete; they use something called a word processor now.

I tried it once and gave up, and I've noticed she's back to handwritten letters, too. We have a computer that is never used, it's also obsolete. It sits there with a towel over it. Never used even once, by either of us, though of course it gets a new towel every once in a while.

I have one of those electronic things that records your calls when you're not in, but it burned a wire or something recently and I haven't replaced it. After all, if you really want to talk to me, you'll try again, won't you? Even if it's long distance? I know you will.

Song in my Head

Have you ever found an old song running through your head, maybe a song you never even liked, and you can't shake it? Wake up in the middle of the night and there it is, words and music, or worse, both words and music only half recalled and there you are, clawing back through the fog trying to remember the foolish words to a tune you never liked in the first place.

Terrible. Happened to me a few nights ago — "Follow the Swallow Back Home" — a simple song of the 1920s we played in the Bayfield Boy's Band in our Indian Pageant of 1924. A World War I veteran named Steinmetz, the original except for looks, of Robert Preston in "The Music Man." Convinced the Town Fathers of Bayfield and Washburn and Ashland, too, that what they desperately needed was a boy's band; and he was the man and he could get the instruments. And he did. I got a brass cornet made in of all places, Czechoslovakia, costing my dad $8. Eight dollars! And if you heard me play it you'd say not a dime over $2.50, but never mind that. Overnight we were the Boy's Band of Bayfield, Wis. And in due time we learned sort of three tunes; "A Hot Time in the Old Town Tonight," (When you hear that Boy's Band on the street, then you'll know that Bayfield has them beat.") "Show Me the Way to Go Home" and "Follow the Swallow," the simple melody that's been driving me nuts the last three days and nights.

"East is East, West is West, I know where the sun shines best Follow the swallow back home."

That's all I can remember of it. So I need your help. Not helping me to remember the rest of the song, helping me forget the part I remember.

Technology is Great...

Bob Hadland called a few minutes ago. "Greg Kinney just died." I'd known Greg at least fifty years, knew he was in bad shape so this unhappy news wasn't unexpected, but still a shock, still a jolt. One more gap in the ranks.

Greg had put, I think he told me, some 35 years in Morty's Bar in Bayfield, as bartender, later as owner. In recent summers, he visited us often at Bark Bay and had a store of backstage stories about tavern life, as anyone in that business is bound to have. But he had kept his counsel. There was a stretch of a year or so, he told me, when Morty had sold the place to a fellow who was sober most of the time, but not all the time, and who now and then would disappear for a week. ("I go on some awful binges," this new owner, George somebody, told me in confidence once). Halfway through one such week, Greg was about to close up when in walks owner, George. "Scotch and soda and a ham sandwich, please."

"We don't serve sandwiches, George."

"That's all right. I've got a little place up in Bayfield; we don't serve sandwiches either."

I suppose over the years, Greg could have blackmailed half the town, but your secrets were safe with him. And the little anecdotes he passed on to us at Bark Bay were at least 30 years old and the people in them long gone. And now he's gone. Rats.

Here in Arizona, the hundred-degree days have dropped into the 70s and 80s and when someone from up north is on the phone and says "It's snowing," we feel pretty smug. Still I miss the winter fun we had as kids and if I ever get back for keeps, I'll be in long johns, a chook, a mackinaw, heavy wool socks and boots every day and maybe enjoy it again. I'll have a constant fire in the fireplace too. My only problem will be Marion "Blades" O'Malley who for 20 years walked to work in Washburn snow and cold and is permanently prejudiced. Never mind, the problem hasn't surfaced yet.

The world of technology we live in leaves me farther behind every day. An ad in this morning's paper says to learn more about their product I have only to click to something. But I have nothing to click and wouldn't know how. Another, full page, says "Visit us online at the Ashley Furniture website, http://www.Ashley furniture.com." Hooboy, lucky we don't need furniture.

Technology is great for people who understand it. I went to the library yesterday, wanted to find a book of John Kennedy's speeches, especially where, during the 1962 Cuban missile crisis, he told Chairman Kruschev, and no argument about it, to back off. Couldn't find the book and don't understand their computers. I finally went to the desk where a young fellow consulted a directory, found the speech and in minutes handed me five neat sheets with every word exactly as spoken forty years ago. Here's the paragraph that saved us: "It shall be the policy of this nation to regard any nuclear missile launched from Cuba against any nation in the Western Hemisphere, as an attack by the Soviet Union on the United States, requiring a full retaliatory response upon the Soviet Union."

It's a wonderful world. Scary though.

There's Copper on them there Beaches

Thinking of buying a boat? This is the best time, when the boys are pulling them out for the winter, that is if there is a best time or even a good time. Having gone through the experience often ("My boat gave me the best days of my life; the day I bought it and the day I sold it.") and now this summer having just done it once again I've found the three-step answer:
1. Get a good local partner
2. Buy the boat
3. Leave town

Following this formula I am now half-owner of a good 22-foot 12-horse IO with Robert "Red" Anderson. He has to drive the 20 miles to Cornie while I'm 2,000 miles away in Phoenix so I think the three of us, Red, myself and the *Drift Away* can sleep well; we won't be bothering each other much. The Driftaway belonged to old friend Bill Bloomer of Cornucopia's Blueberry Lane. Bill died in August on his 87th birthday and will always be missed; Bette wanted someone to buy the boat ("I never really liked that boat") so we did. She said, "Bill would approve." I think he would, too.

Every once in a while someone finds a chunk of pure copper along the shore or in a sand bank; Marion did just that walking the Bark Bay beach this summer. Such pieces are called float copper, I don't know why as they wouldn't. I've hoped to find one all my life — haven't yet — but Roger found one when we were kids digging in the sand bank below our house in Bayfield. About the size of a potato. What became of it? I wish I knew.

There was a bigger one used as a doorstop at the First National Bank — and don't know what happened to that either. They're around somewhere!

Marions' piece weighs almost two pounds and when she picked it up it looked like any other beach rock, black and green. I've just had it acid-washed for $45 and it's beautiful.

I'd give something to know the history of this chunk of pure copper. Maybe I'll learn something from these library books; if I do I'll let you know.

One final word on boats. Years ago I was going to buy the 48-foot Liberty, I don't know why. Julian Nelson said, "I know the Liberty, Hale. The Liberty is an old wooden boat, and anyone who thinks an old wooden boat has improved with age has a wooden head."

I will always be indebted to Julian Nelson.

Those Days are Long Gone, Long Gone

I wrote recently about getting a letter from an old Bayfield classmate Lillian Hanson, Mrs. Roy McCormick (but not to me) in which she enclosed a snapshot of herself taken just a few weeks ago. (Just a minute; I have to trim my nails. These old typewriters insist on very short nails.) Okay, Since Lil and I were in the same grade from Kindergarten on up, graduating with the class of '32, I know her age very well, but in that photo she doesn't look a day over 30.

Rats. Why doesn't she show her years like the rest of us? Just doesn't seem fair. Women.

I may be the only person alive who knows the motto of the Bayfield Class of '32; "Rowing, not Drifting."

There's magic in words, to be sure. Helen Howk suggested, way back then, that our class colors be "Silver and Old Rose" and we voted that in at once. Silver and Old Rose; downright romantic, but in plain English gray and pink. Oh well, that was 68 years ago. We've lived it down.

Choosing the right word counts. Scott Fitzgerald ended *The Great Gatsby* with this beautiful line which, I'm not sure, I think is carved on his gravestone:

"So we beat on, boats against the current, borne back ceaselessly into the past."

Suppose he'd written "So we row on," or "So we paddle on?" "So we beat on" is just right.

Winston Churchill said "I have nothing to offer except blood, toil, tears and sweat." What if he'd said "blood, toil, tears and perspiration?" Puts out the fire, doesn't it? England might have lost the war.

Please excuse my getting so profound, but last week's Police Report in *The County Journal,* usually worth a paragraph, didn't have anything juicy. I'm still wondering, though, as reported some months ago, how that fellow got locked in the post office. I can see getting locked out, but locked in?

Card from old friend and World's Greatest Tuba Player Lou Schindler: "Had a series of audio tests and just as I suspected, I don't hear very well!" Neither do I, and it's awful. You can't keep saying "Eh?", "Say again, please." "Pardon, I didn't quite get that" and so on. Makes people mad.

Here's the trick: just smile and nod, people aren't interested in your response anyway. And if you sense you're being asked a question turn to the fellow next to you and say "What do you think about that, George?"

Works everytime, never mind if his name isn't George.

Biking to the post office this morning I spotted a penny on the street. Did I stop? Would you, for a lousy penny? Walk back to pick it up and bike on? You bet your laughing blue eyes I did.

Anyone who graduated in 1932 and was lucky enough to get a job peeling logs in a box factory for seventeen-and-a-half cents an hour understands. Those days are long gone, long gone, but they never leave you.

Those Herring Look Bigger than I Remember them

Cats. Marion, "Blades," likes to give our cats Irish names, and our current spayed female, Kelly, nearly 10-years old, not my favorite but we get along, prefers sleeping with Blades. Understandable, I do myself. But in the middle of the night, Kelly will come over and thunk down on me. She weighs eight pounds and it's like having someone drop a furry brick on you. She likes to settle in the crook of my knee and I'm expected to instantly freeze, since any movement would disturb her and we can't have that. When I finally do move, she gets up in disgust and plunks down on Blades again. One way or another, the three of us make it through the night. Cats.

I recently wrote five newspapers, two in Hayward, one in La Pointe, plus the Ashland Press and the Milwaukee Journal, asking if they would like to run these Notes From the Horn. Not a word from any of them, not a word, which I suppose is answer enough. Still, I expected at least a postcard saying, "Thanks, but no."

I sent President Bush a card the other day, said merely, "Mr. President, don't do it!," referring to Iraq of course. Knew perfectly well he'd never see that card. But in time I'll get an answer thanking me. He won't have written or even seen that either, but I don't mind. I thought a few million cards like mine might carry some weight, in any case mine will be answered, I know. Common courtesy.

Eric Hjerstedt Sharp and Barbara Brown Meredith write most of the local stories for this paper, which I read more thoroughly than I would if I were there, and as reporters, those two could make it anywhere. I hope they don't realize this and start looking.

I have just re-read Barbara's story on the fall herring fishing, which fifty years ago was a big thing in Bayfield. She gives the full background of Bayfield's fishing industry in that article, and reading it and seeing her photos of Ben Gustafson's Wolverine and Martin Peterson's Twin Disc coming in, you'll scotch any idea you ever had of becoming a commercial fisherman. Not for me, in my best days I was never that tough. Anyway, I grew up on Lake Superior and I don't have to be out there to know how cold it is. In the shot of Joe Duffy with a box of herring, those herring look bigger than I remember them. Maybe they are.

I liked Darrell's story on the little buck he brought in, which delighted his son, Jack, at two-and-a half a dedicated hunter and proud of his dad anytime. I'm somewhat inclined to see hunters the way a deer does but not in this case. That story was heart-warming. For the reception little Jack gave his dad, I'd have shot that deer myself.

Nurses are Too Smart

All right, Washburn beat Bayfield not once, but twice, and badly too. Rats. Nevermind, the thing to do now is to get behind these fellows and root them home. It's a good town, good people, and we should help them right up the ladder, maybe even to the State Championship. Why not? They beat Bayfield didn't they? Well, then.

Now then, I must keep my promise to Jim Miller and Bob Hadland and continue the saga of esophageal cancer treatment. I'm booked for five weeks, Monday - Friday, weekends off, of radiation therapy and as I write, I am just finishing my third week. Radiation is easy. Five buzzing shots, flat on your back, and that's it.

At the close of the first week, they wheeled me into a room packed with medical artillery where a pleasant young doctor explained that he was about to drill a hole in my stomach where I would be fed through a tube, thus bypassing the cancer and sparing me the pain of swallowing. He said nothing about the pain of having a hole drilled into my stomach.

Now on this groaning and moaning business. Don't overplay your hand. That nutritious brown goop they are draining into you looks like Bark Creek after a big storm. (I know the road sign says Bark River, but I grew up with Bark Creek, pronounced crick, and I'm too old to change.) And I have two of the finest, Marion and my little grand-niece, Kathleen O'Malley, answering my every need. Judicious, properly spaced moans are very effective. For awhile, the ladies came running, but I have found a pitiful, barely audible whimper works best. Careful, now. You are dealing with shrewd, skeptical females who know you well, you with your slick talk and city ways, and they will spot a fake moan or whimper a mile off. One fake whimp and you will hear a voice from the TV room, "Yeah, what is it?" You're dead in the water right there.

Probably best to leave out the sympathy whimps and moans entirely. Your nurses are too smart.

NOTES FROM THE HORN

You Want Mysteries?

"A huge new novel, to be welcomed and relished!_Library, Journal_ "Colorful, brilliant, wholly satisfying!"_Publishers Weekly_ "Reverberates with mythical overtones that are rich, deep, and full of compassion for the human condition"_Newsday_

"The Glorious New York Times Best Seller!"_Los Angeles Times._

The Phoenix library here has just come up with a fine idea for peddling books nobody wants. They seal them in neat little paper bags, price $1, set them under a sign saying, No Peeking! And off they go, paperbacks I never heard of written by 13 authors, or maybe the same author with 13 names, plus the quotations above.

Never flicked through such expletive deleted trash in my life but this method of getting rid of it seems to work. If any Bayfield County Librarians want to clean house, here's the answer. Librarians all, you're welcome! I feel this is a public service.

The weekly Sheriff's Report in this paper beats every one of those books all hollow. All the complaints are intriguing and some are miniature mysteries.

Take this one: "At 8:13 p.m. April 24, report of suspicious looking male in Grand View area. Best description complainant could give was that the man looked like a bear, was heavy set, dressed in black, with lots of facial hair. Man had a blue bedroll and knapsack and was walking around Grand View."

Well, probably quite a few Grand View citizens have beards. I know editor Darrell does but he keeps it neatly trimmed. Haven't seen him with bedroll and knapsack, but with all those hunting and fishing trips, not to mention those four horses he keeps having to corral, I wouldn't rule him out.

How about this? Any connection with Grand View bear you think?

"April 29, 7:07 p.m. Male subject locked into the Washburn Post office. Unknown how this happened."

You like mysteries? We got mysteries.

"On April 29, at 1:57 p.m., report from a party who found a bear this morning on the road while out walking that had a rope around its neck. Incident happened about a mile and a half off Long Lake Road. Warden removed the bear from location, and removed a bullet from the bear. The DNR would like anyone who may have seen someone in the area or who heard gunshots to report the incident."

Wow. "Warden removed the bear from location, and removed a bullet from the bear."

For the moment let's forget the bedroll and knapsack. He removed a bullet? Untied the rope around his neck? Moved him to a different location — the Washburn Post Office maybe? I wouldn't dare question a word of this report, but I'll be back here in a few weeks and would kind of like to interview the sheriff. This report needs, shall we say, fleshing out.

Glacial Kettles

Never Mind Birthday Cards: Send Money for the Kettles

In the process of trying to get our glacial kettles recognized as a real attraction — they've been patiently waiting 10,000 years — I'm getting a real education.

I wrote Governor Thompson: there should be a state park. He said, in effect, "I like the idea but it's county land."

I called Sue Black, Director of State Bureau of Parks and Recreation in Madison who sent me an excellent map of glacial activity in Wisconsin (I've since asked for more of them) and politely wrote, "The area is already protected in a County Forest. Beyond its mission of fiber production, the County Forest also has a mission to provide recreation and protect significant resources."

Well, it's good to know where you stand.

At her suggestion I called Phil Wallace, DNR man at Spooner; caught him filleting five big northern pike which he said, "Won't have a bone in 'em when I'm through." No use pursuing the state, he said, the county calls the shots there. "I'll send you the names and addresses of the County Board." He has, the list is just in and I'll make use of it.

Called Patricia Pollack of the Wisconsin Department of Transportation in Superior who passed me on to Marc Bowker of their Traffic Section. Same story. He said, "Sorry, that's a County Road and County Forest. I know where it is though, I'm from Bayfield." I said, "I was born and brought up in Bayfield; does the name O'Malley ring a bell?"

"Nope."

So much for that call.

NOTES FROM THE HORN

Lake Superior GLACIAL KETTLES

A special place in Bayfield County brought to our attention by Hale O'Malley

Mel Clark's sister in West Allis sent me a clipping mentioning a Drew Hanson, "spokesman for the Ice Age Park Trail Foundation," an outfit I'd never heard of. Turns out that while I'm only trying to put up a road sign this volunteer group has been creating a thousand-mile glacial trail zig-zagging through the state and has been at it 40 years!

And I thought I was persistent.

Talked to the Foundation's office manager Tracy Hamley who had Mr. Hanson call me. Very pleasant fellow. He sent me a copy of their publication, a 20-page magazine on four pages of which they don't ask a donation. That's all right; if you're buying up old forties and easements through valuable privately-owned parcels of land you have to pay for them, and if you're doing a thousand miles worth of this I suppose you have to pay a lot.

Their map shows the trail, over half completed Mr. Hanson says, running south from Green Bay almost to Illinois, then north and clear to St. Croix Falls. Won't reach Bayfield County though. Pity.

The Wisconsin Geological Survey has sent me (for $9.50; just paid 'em) the "Pleistocene Geology of the Superior Region, Wisconsin" which is far too technical for me. You have to be a professional geologist. I looked up Pleistocene though — "the first epoch of the quaternary period" — and went out the same door I went in.

Pam Schuler of the National Park Service says she'll send me more Ice Age maps. They're great.

I'm just trying, for starters, to change the name of a road but I don't have 40 years to do it; I'm 83 today. Never mind birthday cards; send money. I'll send it on to the Bayfield County Board and ask them to put up a good sign on the Town Dump Road saying "Glacial Kettle Road," and if there's money left over use it to cut a few trails on the rim of some of those kettles.

Fair enough?

NOTES FROM THE HORN

Awesome Gouges in the Barrens
Nov. 11, 1997

I recently talked with a school teacher who really surprised me with how conversant she was on a variety of odd subjects. "Yes, I'm quite eclectic: "choosing what appears to be the best from diverse sources, systems or styles." It's in the book. Then later I found she didn't know what glacial kettles were!

Well. For those of you who haven't been following these notes (Heavens!): Glacial Kettles are huge potholes in the earth, formed by immense blocks of ice sheared off and pushed down by the advancing glacier centuries ago. Ours are just east of County Trunk C between Cornie and Washburn and you get to them by driving on North Boundary Road or the Town Dump Road (awful name, that. I prefer Glacial Kettle Road or maybe just Glacial Trail. We'll decide later).

There used to be a song called "No One Has Endurance Like the Man who Sells Insurance." I endured some thirty years of that job and if I suddenly had to go back to it I'd send for Dr. Kevorkian. Never mind. You do learn persistence — learn it or starve — and one of these days, one of these days, Washburn and Cornucopia, not to mention Bayfield, Bayfield County and the whole State of Wisconsin, will leave their Glacial Kettle Park with neat signs on the highway leading you in and walking trails around the rim of those awesome gouges in the barrens. Patience, friends, patience and persistence. And endurance.

Let us move on for the moment. My good wife Marion "Blades" O'Malley, born Marion Corning in Washburn some years back knew at once there'd been a big mistake. She was supposed to be born in Arizona. Not an insurmountable problem though since like all Washburn girls she was born smart, and today has a home in Phoenix and on cool days goes further south to Mexico to a little beach house on the Sea of Cortez, and if another ice age moves in will probably trot on down and do a high-wire act on the equator.

She'll take two things with her, the *Wall Street Journal* and a can of WD-40. If I'm lucky she'll take me too, but those two things for sure. For Blades O'Malley life without the *Wall Street Journal* and WD-40 would be hollow indeed.

Forgive me for jumping around here, but an incident from those bad old days selling life insurance 50 years ago door-to-door in the winter in northern Wisconsin — just came back to me. I'd called on an old-timer known in Washburn as "Pete the Plumber" and was shown the door in short order. O.K., that kind of reception comes with the territory. But I made the mistake just a few weeks later of calling on old Pete again and this time got told off in words Darrell wouldn't let me use here.

All right. We now fast-forward some 20 years to my little real estate office in Cornucopia, where one fine morning in comes a grizzled old coot, very pleasant, who speaks as follows: "Mr. O'Malley, I'm Pete Olson. I have a plumbing and well-drilling business in Washburn. I know you're doing some building out here and if we can be of service to you I hope you'll call us."

Suddenly it comes to me — this is the guy who tied the can to me twenty years ago. Ahhh. And here I have him, right in the palm of my hand. I said nothing for a few seconds, savoring the moment. The rest of the conversation I remember exactly; I think you would too. "I remember you very well, Mr. Olson," I said with a smile. "I called on you when I was selling insurance twenty years ago. You weren't very nice to me."

"Well I'll be damned," he said.

We both smiled.

"I'll be glad to call your people anytime we have work for them," I said.

We parted friends. I'd said the right thing and I'm still glad I did. You would be too. I know you would.

WCC Crew at Glacial Kettles

Nice letter just in from David Bratley of Washburn. He had written earlier about the junk at the bottom of our glacial kettles, and now reports: "Thought I'd finally let you know about the cleanup of your glacial kettles. During the last week of May, John Mesko of the Bayfield County Forestry Department, picked up all the broken bits and pieces of porcelain from bathroom and kitchen appliances scattered down the side of the kettle.

He then marked and surrounded all the trees with orange ribbon and contacted the Wisconsin Conservation Corps to do that portion of the cleanup. The WCC crew, under the direction of Don Mead, the regional Team Leader at the Iron River office, removed the tires on July 22, when they took out 25 in all and placed them in a pile where the Bayfield County Forestry Department could pick them up with their trucks and dispose of them. So Hale, your kettles are clean."

Heartening news indeed. He says the stuff hauled out has been there a long time so I can't really take credit for getting this welcome action. Heck, I think I will anyway. He continues, "So please don't give up promoting the kettles. No one was even aware of them before and now they are well known and visited regularly. We visited because of your writings and as a result the kettles wound up getting cleaned up because it was now an important site. By all means, keep these promotions rolling."

My gosh. I'm doing my best to be embarrassed by all this but it isn't easy. Anyway we are going back to Arizona in a few days, too soon as always, and since the glacier never got that far, nobody's ever heard of a glacial kettle. I'll be O.K.. in a week or so.

I Hear More about Glacial Kettles

The County Tourist Department has just forwarded a letter from a fellow in Rice Lake who needed better directions on finding our glacial kettles. I was happy to send him a topographical map and a descriptive folder. I hope he tries again. With the fall foliage thinned, this is the right time of year, though we will always need some trimming and should have a walking trail around the rim of at least the deepest earth gouge. Would cost very little.

A few more letters like that, plus backers like Dave Bratley, whose efforts got the old tires and hardware cleaned out and we will get somewhere.

There will be a Glacial Kettle Road

Since the Town Board turned down my offer to pay for a "Glacial Kettle Road" sign I want to be sure you know how to get there. Easy. From Washburn take County C exactly 13 miles, turn right. There's your road. From Cornie six miles, turn left. Drive 2.3 miles to the gravel pit, park, walk a few steps to some of the largest kettles in Wisconsin, 200 feet deep, which has been waiting 10,000 years to meet you. There. We ain't dead yet.

NOTES FROM THE HORN

Hale O'Malley

Other Savage Press Books

OUTDOORS, SPORTS & RECREATION

Cool Fishing for Kids 8-85
 by Frankie Paul and "Jackpine" Bob Cary
Curling Superiority! by John Gidley
Dan's Dirty Dozen by Mike Savage
The Duluth Tour Book by Jeff Cornelius
The Final Buzzer by Chris Russell

ESSAY

Battlenotes: Music of the Vietnam War by Lee Andresen
Hint of Frost, Essays on the Earth by Rusty King
Hometown Wisconsin by Marshall J. Cook
Potpourri From Kettle Land by Irene I. Luethge

FICTION

Burn Baby Burn by Mike Savage
Charleston Red by Sarah Galchus
Keeper of the Town by Don Cameron
Lake Effect by Mike Savage
Mindset By Enrico Bostone
Off Season by Marshall J. Cook
Something in the Water by Mike Savage
The Year of the Buffalo by Marshall J. Cook
Voices From the North Edge by St. Croix Writers
Walkers in the Mist by Hollis D. Normand

NOTES FROM THE HORN

REGIONAL HISTORY, HUMOR, MEMOIR

Beyond the Freeway by Peter J. Benzoni
Crocodile Tears and Lipstick Smears by Fran Gabino
Fair Game by Fran Gabino
Some Things You Never Forget by Clem Miller
Stop in the Name of the Law by Alex O'Kash
Superior Catholics by Cheney and Meronek
Widow of the Waves by Bev Jamison

BUSINESS

Dare to Kiss the Frog by vanHauen, Kastberg & Soden
SoundBites by Kathy Kerchner, Second Edition

POETRY

Appalachian Mettle by Paul Bennett
Eraser's Edge by Phil Sneve
Gleanings from the Hillsides by E.M. Johnson
*In the Heart of the Fores*t by Diana Randolph
Moments Beautiful Moments Bright by Brett Bartholomaus
Nameless by Charlie Buckley
Pathways by Mary B. Wadzinski
Philosophical Poems by E.M. Johnson
Poems of Faith and Inspiration by E.M. Johnson
The Morning After the Night She Fell Into the Gorge
    by Heidi Howes
Thicker Than Water by Hazel Sangster
Treasured Thoughts by Sierra
Treasures from the Beginning of the World by Jeff Lewis

SOCIAL JUSTICE

Throwaway People: Danger in Paradise by Peter Opack

SPIRITUALITY

Life's Most Relevant Reality by Rod Kissinger, S.J.
Proverbs for the Family by Lynda Savage, M.S.
The Awakening of the Heart by Jill Downs
The Hillside Story by Pastor Thor Sorenson

OTHER BOOKS AVAILABLE FROM SP

Blueberry Summers by Lawrence Berube
Beyond the Law by Alex O'Kash
Dakota Brave by Howard Johnson
Jackpine Savages by Frank Larson
Spindrift Anthology by The Tarpon Springs Writer's Group
The Brule River, A Guide's Story by Lawrence Berube
Waterfront by Alex O'Kash